They Have Forgotten Us

They Have Forgotten Us

The Working Class,

Care, and the Looming Crisis

Peter Mertens

Translated from the Finnish by
Erika Ulrix, Walter De Muyter and Jan Reyniers

First published in July 2021 by
1804 Books at The People's Forum, New York, NY
in association with
LeftWord Books, New Delhi, India

Originally published in Finnish, 2020

Original Finnish © Peter Mertens
US copyright 2021 © 1804 Books at The People's Forum, New York, NY
India copyright 2021 © LeftWord Books

ISBN: 978-1-7368500-1-5 (paperback)
        978-81-950310-1-6 (ebook)

All Rights reserved. No part of this book may be reproduced or transmitted in any form or by any means, electronic or mechanical, including photo-copying, recording or any information storage retrial system without permission in writing from the publisher, except brief passages for review purposes.

Contents

Preface to the English Edition — 7
Preface — 15

PART I
Heroes — 19
You Don't See the Stars Until it Gets Dark — 24
COVID-19 is a Class Virus — 27
The Invisibles — 38
The Sleeping Giant is Awake — 46

PART II
Care — 53
The Silver Market — 61
Every Ounce of Prevention is Worth
   a Pound of Cure — 64
Pandemics are Pivotal Moments — 70
The Asian Approach — 74
Rather a Body Cream than a Vaccine — 79
Could You Patent the Sun? — 83

PART III
The Looming Crisis — 89
When the Mayor of New York Quotes Karl Marx — 94
A Tinderbox That Can Set the Prairie on Fire — 98
'Nothing is More Permanent than the Temporary' — 100
Is All That Money Going to Those Who Need It? — 107
A Plan Like the One Proposed by
   Alexandria Ocasio-Cortez — 112
The Prometheus Plan — 116
Making Circumstances Human — 123

Preface to the English Edition

With this English edition, *They Have Forgotten Us* is being published in its fifth language (after Dutch, French, German, and Spanish). For that, I am extremely grateful to LeftWord Books (in particular Vijay Prashad, Winnie Chauhan, and Deby Veneziale).

There was a time when books were read for hours on end. In these bombastic Twitter times, this is less evident. Since writing the book, seven months have flown by. In the life of a virus, that's an eternity. By comparison, between the initial contamination with SARS-CoV-2 and the global lockdown lie a mere seven weeks. Today, we have seen two waves, ninety million infections, and more than two million deaths. There were lockdowns, relaxations, and more lockdowns. Exceptional measures were called 'provisional', and then 'temporary', and then the temporary exception gradually became a regime.

When the book was published, Western opinion makers frowned. What do you mean a class virus? King, emperor, cardinal, all of them get corona, right? Tell that to the donkey. COVID-19 has sharpened all the contradictions of global capitalism, the facts have exposed the truth.

In the dark night of this pandemic, those with vital occupations continued to work. These were not the hedge fund managers, the stock market traders, the financial consultants, or talk show luminaries. Rather, they were nurses, garbage collectors, cleaning ladies, teachers, shelf stackers, postal workers, and bus drivers. They took the risks and kept things running. They still do. But as soon as the curves go down, the chattering class demands that we forget all about their sacrifice. Quickly the amnesia sets in, and the calls to go back to the impossible status quo before the virus get louder. 'When they were scared of dying, all of a sudden we all became heroes. But now, they have already forgotten us,' Monica from Cremona, Italy, says in the book.

Winners and Losers

Noah, a friend from the Netherlands, ordered my book online. It was delivered to him by a Bol.com driver who earns barely two euros per delivery. Bol.com is an online retailer, the Dutch version of Amazon. The owners of Bol.com are among the winners of the crisis. Their net profit has doubled to over two billion euros. On the other side of the story, exploited couriers deliver the goods to the customer for meagre wages. In gigantic distribution centres, order pickers walk up to twenty kilometres a day and assemble 225 packages an hour for barely ten euros gross. They are people of all nationalities. They shack up in living containers on the Bol.com camping site and pay 400 euros for a single mattress. These are the Netherlands in 2021; this is modern slavery.

Jeff Bezos, the largest shareholder of Amazon, that other parcel giant, is one of the richest people in the world. During the corona crisis, he became seventy-eight billion dollars richer while his shelf stackers struggled to make ends meet. That COVID-19 is a democratic virus that affects everyone equally is the biggest lie of 2020. The rich get richer, the poor get poorer. This virus is indeed a class virus. "Mertens calls the coronavirus a class virus," writes the German weekly *Unsere Zeit*. 'He is analyzing the impact of the pandemic across Europe. It affects the weakest and poorest in all countries. In a precarious work situation, health and safety are also precarious. Take for instance the seasonal workers on the vegetable plantations in southern Europe or the contract workers of meat giant Tönnies in Germany.'

Class virus: that phrase is central to just about every international review of the book: One finds it in the magazine *Jacobin* in the US; in the French *L'Humanité*; in the German newspapers junge *Welt*, *Neues Deutschland*, and *Unsere Zeit* ; in the Dutch newspaper *NRC Handelsblad*; and on the Spanish news sites of *Cuarto Poder* and *El Plural*. Class virus. What else could Gabriela Bucher, managing director of Oxfam International, say when she presented her inequality report: 'We stand to witness the greatest rise in inequality since record keeping began.' What happened between 18 March and 31 December 2020? On the one hand, the number of people living in poverty in the world increased up to 500 million. On the other hand, the ten richest inhabitants of the planet saw their wealth increase by no less than 540 billion dollars. Digest that! The increase in the wealth of these ten richest people on earth is enough to vaccinate the entire world population, and to ensure that no one ends up in poverty. 'The deep divide between the rich and poor is as deadly as the virus,' Gabriela Bucher concludes.

Throughout the world, the poorest regions have a higher infection and mortality rate than the economically more prosperous regions. In England, mortality rates due to COVID-19 in the poorest neighbourhoods are twice as high as in the richer ones. The same goes for India, France, and Spain.

Does Big Pharma Also Have Patent Rights to a Whole Pack of Politicians?

Barely a few milliliters of water-like liquid in a glass bottle, it doesn't seem particularly impressive, a vaccine like that. But make no mistake. Those few milliliters of liquid contain a huge amount of knowledge. The magic potion of the 'druid Panoramix' from the Asterix comics is nothing compared to it. The small nothingness in the bottle is based on all kinds of findings from a range of scientific disciplines: from cell biology to physiology, from immunology to epidemiology, from physics to statistics.

So, it is fantastic that today we have workable vaccines that can stop the virus. Will everyone get a spoon from the jar of Panoramix, so that we can defeat the Romans? No. This will take years. Why? Because not enough vaccines are being produced, they say. Can't we produce more? Of course, we can! Technically it is perfectly possible. Then why isn't it happening? Because it's not allowed. The vaccines are covered by patent protection, and so not everyone is allowed to produce them. Can you imagine anything more absurdly horrific?

Reality Check. Hundreds of thousands of people worldwide die from the virus, hospitals groan under the weight of the pandemic, entire economic sectors are brought to a standstill, businesses go bust, people lose their jobs, and young people lose hope. But... we're not going to solve that any time soon, because Big Pharma won't let us.

Reality check, *again*. If we wanted to, tomorrow tens of thousands of companies around the world could switch to producing vaccines. If we do so by the end of 2021, we will be able to inoculate the entire population of this blue planet. It would be great for the people, for health, and for the economy. But it isn't happening, because one monopoly sector is standing in the way: the pharmaceutical industry.

It seems that Big Pharma not only patents vaccines, but has also patent rights on the whole pack of politicians everywhere. Instead of taking responsibility and insisting on the production of a sufficient number of vaccines, the political caste limits itself to parroting the pharmaceutical lobby. The patents allegedly exist because the scientific knowledge in those little glass vials of vaccine was developed by private giants. Humbug and poppycock! All workable vaccines are built on years of scientific research in publicly funded laboratories and research institutions. I wrote that last summer in this book and it has since been confirmed. Taxpayers and public governments are pumping massive amounts of money into vaccine development. But there is no return on that investment.

The War for a Few Milliliters of Aqueous Liquid

The mRNA vaccines from Pfizer and Moderna are based on fundamental research carried out at an American university. AstraZeneca in turn partnered with Oxford University. In the final race of 2020, the US government invested more than ten billion dollars in developing a vaccine. The European Union also had six billion euros of public money at its disposal. BioNTech, the company that joined forces with Pfizer, received almost 400 million euros from the German government. *Danke schön.*

There should have been a demand for the research results to be made available for the public so that the vaccine could have been rapidly produced worldwide. The failure to do so is criminal. As a result, in the coming months too few vaccines will be available to protect the majority of the globe and some countries will have to wait for years. Only a handful of companies will be able to supply the vaccines and any hitch will immediately cause major delays.

'We are stuck with a European Commission that is more likely to demand its member states reduce pensions and public spending, than to demand the pharmaceutical companies deliver the vaccines they have promised,' the well-known Spanish journalist Pascual Serrano wrote earlier this year. In the Belgian Parliament, Dr Sofie Merckx, MP for the Workers' Party of Belgium (PTB) added: 'Today we vaccinate not to the rhythm of the people's needs, but to the rhythm of the profit hungry pharmaceutical companies.' Pfizer, meanwhile, announced that the corona vaccine will account for fifteen billion dollars in new sales, resulting in an astonishing five billion dollars in profits.

Soon, millions of doses of the vaccine will roll off the conveyor belt of the South African company Aspen. However, it is feared that South Africans themselves will have to wait another four years for the vaccine. Rich countries have been buying up 'the supply'. They bought double or triple the quantities required. 'The market fails to organize an equitable distribution according to health needs. This would require solidarity,' rightly concludes Belgian professor of Family Medicine, Jan De Maeseneer.

The sacred promise of making the corona vaccine a public good available to all has long been broken. Whoever ordered first and paid the most – especially the latter – will have the upper hand. In contrast, more than seventy countries may be left empty-handed this year: they will have no vaccines. A young man from a rich country is more likely to be vaccinated than an older woman from a poorer country, even though she has a much higher mortality risk. Not only is this fundamentally unjust, but it is also unbearably short-sighted. As long as the pandemic rages, everyone is unsafe. And the longer the virus is around, the more variants become possible and the greater the chance that the new vaccines will be inadequate. In Europe, authentic left-wing parties, trade unions, NGOs and citizens joined forces to launch the European citizens' initiative Right2Cure. Via the website www.noprofitonpandemic.eu they want to collect one million signatures to pressure the European Commission to abolish the patents on corona vaccines. 'It's time to open up vaccine patents,' says initiator Anne Delespaul, general practitioner at Medicine for the People, the Belgian network of people's health centres.

Towards a Global Mindquake

Too little, too late, too non-transparent, too expensive, governments everywhere are lagging behind. It's not the first time they failed. The face masks' catastrophe was followed by shortages of oxygen and protective clothing. Afterwards, we had the tragedies in the homes for the elderly and the complete failure of testing and tracing. And today, we are unable to vaccinate quickly and efficiently. Recurring failure is not an exception. There's a pattern behind it.

This pattern is a sacred belief in the free market and in capitalism. 'The only wheels which political economy sets in motion are greed, and the war amongst the greedy—competition.' Karl Marx wrote that many years ago, and no one has ever proven him wrong.. The entire social order has been arranged and set up to let a few large corporations call the shots, while all the facts are screaming in our faces that a public and collective approach is vital. The ties between politics and the pharmaceutical lobby should be broken. We must invest not only in public research, but also in the production of medicines. There is a need to redefine the entire health care system. We refuse to see care as a commercial playground for large corporations; care is a basic necessity for every community. We see health care not merely as curative, on the contrary, it should put a premium on prevention in order to avoid as much illness and deprivation as possible.

In this pandemic, a lot of people in the hospitals and elderly care centres have provided the best care with the resources available. 'But our preventive health care system is much weaker,' says well-known Belgian infectologist, Erika Vlieghe. 'It's no coincidence,' she says, 'that countries like Cuba, Vietnam, and Thailand are managing this crisis more effectively.'

All those countries have a strongly developed preventive care system, close to the people. While writing this book I spoke with Minister K.K. Shailaja, the popular communist health minister of the Indian state of Kerala. Kerala has relatively fewer COVID-19 victims. The secret lies in the district health centres. Every neighbourhood has one. And everyone can go there. These centres employ 26,000 prevention workers, mostly women. They know everyone in the neighbourhood, and at the slightest corona contamination they nip the outbreak in the bud. What a contrast with a rich country like Belgium. Also in Cuba, it is the same; there too prevention is paramount. Moreover, Cubans help where they can. In full lockdown, medical brigades from Cuba were building a field hospital in Italy. A small country from the South helping a rich country from the North. 'We are not heroes,' the Cubans say, 'We just share what we have.' For the free-marketeers, that's too radical. For humanity, that should be normal. As far as I am concerned, Cuban doctors deserve the Nobel Peace Prize.

COVID-19 may be a tipping point. Much more important than the great earthquake of Lisbon in 1755 was the 'mindquake' that followed, writes Philipp Blom. That 'mindquake' challenged prevailing thinking. We should do, at least as much today. We should want to help set the agenda and define the themes of the debate. We should talk about the fact that the market does not work. We should talk about the fact that thousands of people starve today while stock markets are going through the roof. We should talk about the fact that we have already injected 4 trillion euros of public money into the economy to get the engine going and that it was barely ten years ago, during the banking crisis, that we also did this. We should talk about what this reveals about the alleged superiority of the self-regulating market, that it has to receive thousands of billions of euros from all of us every ten years.

'If people can land on the moon, why can't we solve compelling problems on Earth?' asks Italian economist Mariana Mazzucato. We need ambitious public targets. '*Moonshots*' she calls them, missions. We need: access to health and education for all, a public supply of clean energy, quality and accessible public transport, a society without a digital gap, with public data carriers and free WIFI. All those ambitions are less utopian than landing on Mars, and that landing was successful. However, we will have to stand up to the vested interests of big capital.

We have to stress that too. Because today we pump trillions into the system, but all that money flows almost directly to the greedy capitalists of Big Pharma, to the fossil fuel giants, to the tech giants who eat away at our privacy or to the speculators on the stock exchange, just like after the banking crisis. That's not a solution. As we free ourselves from the virus, we must also free ourselves from the large private tentacles that control the earth. The *moonshots* we need are not those that let the private giants control society's priorities. It is time for a change, it is time for public initiative in producing and organising energy, transport, digital technology, and care.

'The mind that opens to a new idea never returns to its original size,' said Albert Einstein. The time has come.

Brussels, 31 January 2021

Preface

Urbain, my friend, this one is for you.

On this cool evening of 13 March 2020, I am paying a visit to Urbain. He is lying in department three on the first floor of the AZ Nikolaas in Sint-Niklaas. This is the Oncology Department. His white hair is sticking out from all sides and he is wearing a delicate pair of spectacles with round lenses. I don't think I have ever seen those glasses before. To me, this makes Urbain look a bit like Einstein, but I don't say it because Flanders' Minister-President Jan Jambon is speaking far too loud through the neighbour's TV set behind the curtain. The Prime Minister is not my priority right now.

Urbain, my father-in-law, is dying and I am speechless. It is dark outside when I leave. In early March, the sun goes to bed early. On the ground floor of the hospital, a woman is cordoning off the entrance and placing a very ugly sign: Caution! COVID-19.

I'll never see Urbain again. I am not allowed to see him anymore. I did not know that. Lockdown goes into effect on that very evening. Only Nadine and Frank are allowed to visit their father. Nobody else is permitted, not even the grandchildren. Sons-in-law certainly not, the many pints I used to enjoy in Urbain's company do not count.

Urbain Peeters passed away on Friday evening, 3 April 2020, at 7:20 PM. Not as a result of Covid-19, but from the effects of nicotine, just like my father ten years ago.

Only fifteen people are allowed to be present at the funeral service. Aunt Lea is not allowed to attend. Urbain's friends from the Thalamus' bar are not allowed to be present either. We are standing there, the fifteen of us, awfully far apart, under a large green weeping willow in the Kruibeke Cemetery. The man from the funeral home calls it the Friedhof. Friedhof, that's much nicer than cemetery. It means peace garden.

I just don't like the idea of a funeral without a wake. On our way home we hear on the radio that the measures have to be applied 'strictly'. The rule being that only children are allowed to say goodbye. And the rules apply to all. An exception is made, though, when it comes to producing gearboxes in a factory. That's okay. Producing garden furniture in a production unit where sixty to seventy people are working together, that is also allowed. However, more than fifteen people at a funeral service is not allowed. Such is the rule. It is our civic duty to stay at home, to produce, and to shut up. I miss Urbain.

Back home from the peace garden, I know it for sure: I will be getting everything off my chest in writing, but I'm having a drink first. I'm more of a 'Westmalleman', whereas Urbain was a 'Leffeman'. And this is why I drink a brown Leffe in homage to Urbain, a Leffe in homage to life.

Urbain, my friend, this one is for you.

We will not forget anything, and no one.

They Have Forgotten Us

PART I

Heroes

I must admit I'm a bit of a hypochondriac,
every other night I ask my wife to check
whether my forehead is hot.
But that's not the issue at stake. I'm not afraid of getting ill.
What is it that makes me afraid, then?
I'm afraid to discover
that the civilization I know is just a house of cards.
That everything will be wiped out.
But I also fear the opposite to come true:
that once the fear is gone, everything will be as before.
Paolo Giordano, 'How Contagion Works'

St. Peter's Hospital, Brussels. The black Mercedes is moving at an exasperatingly slow speed. For the first time since the outbreak of the Corona crisis, the Prime Minister is going to visit the front line. Green tents are set-up along the driveway to the hospital. In recent months, they served as an emergency hospital, a hospital for the hospital. Healthcare providers are standing in an endless row in front of the emergency tents. They are waiting. As soon as Prime Minister Sophie Wilmès' Mercedes approaches, they turn their backs on her, one after the other. They are silent. They stand in deadly silence. 'Politicians, too, are constantly turning their backs on us when we are asking for help,' says a nurse from the socialist trade union. 'Our teams are understaffed and the number of burnouts is growing. We demand a re-evaluation of our profession and an increase in the number of staff.' The pictures of the silent, sturdy white backs are being seen worldwide. The BBC, as well as Reuters and El Universal, are all reporting on the action.

'Silent protest is just so powerful,' the Indian newspaper *The Indian Express* headlines.

The reason why the pictures of the turned backs were seen around the world is because healthcare personnel worldwide identify with this action. 'No more cheers, let's all get together.' No more cheers, the time has come for social action. Such were the words also heard in Paris in early summer. In June, the workers and professionals in the French healthcare sector were present in no less than 250 demonstrations. Geriatrists, maintenance staff, anaesthetists, doctors, administrative staff, healthcare workers, kitchen staff, nurses, volunteers, radiologists, and the other '-ists', all of them have joined in. Nathalie Ritz, a nurse in the Paris region, is fed up. She has come with her colleagues to express her anger under the banner of 'Ni nonne, ni conne, ni bête de somme'! Neither a nun, nor a fool, nor a slave. 'We are not asking for a medal or a petty thank-you bonus. We demand a decent wage.'

'Heroes today, forgotten tomorrow?' questions a banner carried by nurses in Berlin. Healthcare workers have saved countless lives all over the planet, and that is what they continue doing. This has often happened at the cost of their own lives. In early July, Amnesty International reported that at least three thousand health workers worldwide had died from the effects of the Coronavirus. That number may well be a serious underestimation.

In spite of being understaffed, our hospitals did a great job in the midst of the Corona crisis. In Belgium, we have not been confronted with US conditions such as overcrowded hospital corridors, the inevitable selection among patients as to who receives treatment, or refrigerated vans lined up to take the corpses away. Lessons have been quickly learnt from the Italian drama: special Covid-19 wards, extra beds in intensive care units, downgraded chronic care, and separated patient flows. Both the tenacity and dedication of staff and management have worked miracles.

Working in healthcare is one of the most beautiful things on earth. It is human work. You are looking after sick people who are suffering and struggling, people in pain or in fear, begging or thankful. People who are placing their hopes in your hands. That's what you're dealing with. However, due to a shortage of colleagues, a lack of resources, of time, of respect, such commitment is often impossible to fulfill. 'I would love to have time for a chat with the man who is never asking for anything, the one lying at the end of the hallway,' Sandra says. The workload in the geriatrics' ward where she is working is too high. This is harmful to the man who is never asking for anything, but it is also harmful to Sandra. She wants to do her damn job well. That's from where she gets her satisfaction. When that is no longer possible, many of those like Sandra just hang their white coats back on the hook.

Things have been simmering in healthcare for a long time and this little virus is now making the pot boil over quickly, splashing everywhere. Wherever the actions were undertaken by the white coats in June, they were much bigger than expected. This is a serious matter. They have moved mountains; they have not counted their hours; and they have been working through the nights, as have the cleaners, the kitchen staff, and the technicians. But you cannot butter your bread with applause. The time has come to translate respect into a larger budget. 'Over the past few months, people have been making a tremendous effort. There have been no resignations from staff members, quite to the contrary. Everybody wanted to be present during that tough period. The commitment has been tremendous,' says a trade unionist from Bellegem. 'Today we are campaigning because small talk is not going to fill any gaps. Belgium is at the bottom of the ladder in Europe in terms of the number of nurses per bed. Reduce the pressure of work by recruiting more people and make the profession more attractive this way. We need additional resources.'

Healthcare costs have been seen as a 'burden' for years. According to the rules of 'political correctness', savings had to be found. In spite of the demographic ageing and a growing need for care, in spite of the increase in chronic diseases and an ever more complex and expensive healthcare system, the previous Di Rupo government reduced the healthcare budget's annual growth ceiling from 4.5 percent to a mere 3 percent. Subsequently, the government further lowered that ceiling to a maximum of 1.5 percent. According to estimates from the Christian mutual health organisations, Belgium's care budget has been structurally reduced by two billion euros over the past five years, constituting a major blow. For some, however, this is not enough. In early January, during the endless government negotiations, Bart De Wever again suggested decreasing the healthcare budget by 5.2 billion euros. That was just a couple of months prior to the COVID-19 crisis exploding in Europe.

'Faced with the fear of dying, they suddenly made all of us heroes. Today they have forgotten about us once again.' says Monica Mariotti stung by her government's insults. 'Soon we'll be seen again as lazy and excessively expensive people wiping patients' behinds.' She is a nurse in the intensive care unit in the severely affected Italian town of Cremona. 'Times are much tougher now than during the peak. In those days we had an enemy to fight. Now, we have some time to think. I just feel lost, hopeless.' At the peak, they were overwhelmed; they had no time for brooding. But as the curves fell, so did the adrenaline. 'I am suffering from insomnia and I have nightmares,' says Monica. 'I wake up a good ten times at night with shortness of breath while my heart is pounding like mad.'

The resilience of the healthcare sector, however, is strong. 'Have they forgotten about us? If so, let them hear us!' From Mexico City to Manila, from Johannesburg to Oslo, 'the front line' is moving into battle. A class struggle led by the indispensable, the unseen. A struggle that could set in motion a wider emancipation movement.

'No, we are not heroes,' says Caroline Fiat, 'we are healthcare workers. We just want to be appreciated for what we are doing. A hero is someone who wears underwear over his tights, not someone in a white coat. If they had done what was needed over the past two years, no heroes would be needed today. We would be well-informed; we would have a sufficient number of staff members and sufficient equipment at our disposal to deal with this crisis.' Three years ago, in 2017, Caroline Fiat made history. She became the first elected healthcare professional ever to sit in the French National Assembly, a working mom. How many times did she campaign with one of her children in the pram? She could not always afford a babysitter. 'In parliament, they just looked down on what I said,' she recounted. 'Do you know what the Health Minister told me? He said: "I can understand that you don't grasp it all." I am working in the healthcare sector, for God's sake!' This is how denigrating the expensive-word chatters are; how disdainful they are toward those in the field who have the real knowledge. 'They have never taken me seriously. However, everything I predicted about healthcare is now happening.'

They've never taken us seriously: it is a widespread feeling throughout the working class.

You Don't See the Stars Until it Gets Dark

You don't see the stars until it gets dark. When the crisis occurred, it suddenly turned dark, very dark. Now you can see the stars better.

If there is one thing we have come to know, it is who really keeps our society going. It is not the overpaid CEOs, the tycoons, or the tax accountants. Year after year they have told us that they are here to ensure our prosperity – nonsense! It is the working class that keeps things going, ordinary working men and women. The people who never appear on talk shows or on opinion pages, except when it is through others talking 'about them'. Those who spend every day selling their labour – filling the shelves, unloading the trucks, washing the bed sheets, taking care of the elderly, picking the strawberries, servicing the shops, boning the carcasses, collecting the waste, running the factories, putting out the fires, cleaning the corridors, and caring for the toddlers. Without all these people, we would not survive a pandemic. We would not be taken care of; we would not have anything to eat; and we would not be safe. While they are forced to expose themselves daily to the virus, they also provide evidence of the yawning gap that exists between the valuation of their work on the market – a meagre wage – and the social value of their activity; they are indispensable.

The official figures released by the European Union during the pandemic indicate that close to one third of the working class is engaged in an 'essential' profession. Education, agriculture and food, science and technology, and care and cleaning are the most important sectors, but by no means the only ones. 'For a long time, it was thought that robots and technology would replace humans at work,' said Professor of Sociology of Labour Mateo Alaluf. 'This crisis has made us realize that human work remains essential.

However, those standing at the end of the payroll line will always be required to be the first in line for chores. The people who earn the least are making our society run.' The professor concludes: 'This crisis has resulted in a further increase in inequalities and has made class differences more noticeable still.'

In the United States, such contrasts are even more pronounced. In the US, thousands of fast-food workers, farm labourers, and meat processors have come to depend on food stamps, processing food during the day and queuing at the food bank in the evening. Lots of bus drivers, cleaners, warehousemen, parcel handlers, garbage collectors, and home-care workers are in the same boat. These low-wage workers have often taken the highest risks. They have been rushed into the line of fire as 'essential' workers in order to take care of people, to feed them, and to protect them. 'We are not essential at all. We are just being sacrificed. If I were to die on the job, I would just be replaced. I have no masks and no gloves. All I've got is a stupid blue jacket from Walmart.' This is what cashier Jennifer Suggs told a New Orleans radio station. They are the heroes of the crisis vs. the 'scum' of capitalism. In normal times, these heroes face blatant exploitation by bosses and patrons as well as contempt from the political class. 'They Killed My Father' is a book written by Edouard Louis about this issue.

COVID-19 exacerbated this exploitation and brought to light that the working class does exist; and what is more, it is essential. It makes it all run. It is being cheered. The class of people who go to work every morning without asking too many questions is suddenly asking itself a lot of questions. Why should I have to choose between health and work? Why can't I enjoy healthy working conditions? How can one argue it is too unsafe to come out of the house unless it is to go to work? Is it necessary for my job to be maintained while the curve is sky-rocketing? Why are so many measures taken against gatherings on the streets while we have to go through the same gate by the hundreds at every shift change? We are taking care of society, but who is taking care of us?

The more the usefulness of the working class becomes clear, the more does the uselessness of the chattering class. If there is one thing people with status, high wages, public recognition, and TV coverage are lacking, it is usefulness to society at large. The words used by French Professor Gérard Mauger are even sharper: 'This pandemic has shown how useless the idle class is, the class that produces nothing at all, that of traders, managers, consultants and advisors of all kinds, specialists in communication, and other sellers of thin air.'

COVID-19 is a Class Virus

'Hello, Peter. I'm a cleaner. One day I have to work for people who have three coughing children on the couch. The next day I have to work at a 90-plus little lady's place. When I raise this issue with my employer, I am told that the clients have been informed about the risks involved. Upon enquiry, however, it appears that this is not the case. All too often we are getting half measures, half-truths, and complete lies. Greetings, Tine.'

When the first lockdown measures were taken in March, Jan Jambon wanted the domestic helpers to continue working. 'Surely you can stay upstairs on the first floor while the cleaning lady is busy downstairs?' he said. With these words, the Minister-President of Flanders unintentionally gave us a clear picture of the Belgian class structure: while the cleaners have to continue working on the lower levels of life, the elite safely withdraw to the upper levels.

The place we call home is not the same for everyone. A small flat is not a villa in Brasschaat. Four whining children in a flat are harder to manage than those same children would be in a house with a big garden. Lying awake all night due to a loss of income weighs more heavily when savings are limited or non-existent. We were not equal before the pandemic broke out, neither are we equal during the pandemic.

'The longer we must stay at home, the naughtier my little brother of six is getting. He does not do his homework and he is very troublesome. Sometimes my Dad dares to be tough on him with us watching helplessly. My parents are much more stressed than usual,' an eleven-year-old girl testifies. She's not the only one. During the crisis, 44,000 children have been interviewed in the Flanders region. One out of every two children says that there is a lot of quarrelling at home right now. One out of ten has experienced physical or verbal violence at home. Half of them are now subject to more school-related stress. One out of four feels that home is too busy a place to do schoolwork, and one out of seven has no place at all to settle down quietly. In families with financial problems, forty-four percent of the children have no one to help them with their schoolwork. In the case of their peers in other families without these financial issues, the figure is twenty-one percent. Walls may conceal a lot, yet inequality is ubiquitous.

The situation at the workplace is not the same for all either. 'My husband has to keep working. He is a welder mechanic. Well now, is that essential? He visits different companies and is scared because we have two high-risk cases in isolation at our home. Surely our health is more important than a piece of iron?' This is what Chantal is e-mailing me. But the head of the Federation of Enterprises in Belgium (FEB), Pieter Timmermans, is happy to explain: 'I would even go so far as to say that the place where you work is likely to be the safest place for you not to get infected.'

When a dismayed journalist confronts the boss of bosses with the fact that both in the distribution sector and among health care personnel people have become infected in the workplace, Timmermans answers: 'You cannot prove that. There is no way of knowing whether a worker was infected at work or in the evening.'

Case closed for Timmermans and his associates. Working is safe. Tell us why? Because I say so! The extensive study conducted at the University of Antwerp proves exactly the opposite. The survey carried out among as many as 80,000 subjects indicates that half of the infections are probably contracted in the workplace. This is also clear from my mailbox. It is literally jam-packed. Dawud writes, 'Hi Peter, what about the employees in call centres? There are 100 of us crammed shoulder to shoulder on the work floor. We could work from home, but the bosses don't want that. All we have is moist Dettol wipes. Who is thinking of us?' At the very moment the FEB was declaring production to be safe, most people on the work floor did not even have enough protective equipment, protective mouthpieces, and appropriate work clothing.

Kelly writes, 'At Family Care we still have no protection: no mouth masks, no hand gel, no protective suits. Nothing.'

It is also impossible to keep a distance of one and a half metres in many sectors. 'My husband works in the industrial sector,' writes Lieve. 'Six people sit in a tiny van from the canteen to the job. In the canteen, they do not even have enough room to sit one metre apart. My husband is not the type to call a doctor for a simple cough. Nothing is said about factory workers. They just keep toiling away with the hope of not becoming infected.'

Nothing is said about factory workers. They're not taken into account. Sciensano, a government agency responsible for keeping data on COVID-19, does not register the professions of patients. In Great Britain, however, the National Statistical Service does just that. In Great Britain, a high level of excess mortality has been registered among the 'essential professions'; particularly in professions where people are in close contact with others. The workplace is by no means the safe haven employers are depicting, quite the contrary.

British researchers have determined that the death toll due to COVID-19 was the highest among guards, cab drivers, bus drivers, truck drivers, foremen, salesmen, shop workers, construction workers, the service professions, as well as hospital suppliers, kitchen staff, catering workers, and waiters. '[…]Precisely in those professions, often the worst paid, with the hardest working conditions, and the most precarious statutes', the researchers write. High-risk jobs are the least paid. COVID-19 is a class virus with low paid workers on the front line.

'This is an important report. It establishes that COVID-19 is largely an occupational disease in the working population. It does not only concern healthcare and social workers, but it also concerns many other professions involving human contacts,' says Neil Pearce. He is a Professor of Epidemiology and Biostatistics.

He goes on to state: 'The highest risk is to be found in jobs that require interaction with the public. This is hardly surprising at all. You don't need to have a university degree in mathematics to understand that driving a bus involves constant contact with the public, often without the right protective equipment. And that this makes you more vulnerable to the virus.' French researchers came to the same conclusion. Low-skilled workers who come into frequent contact with the public are the ones most affected by the virus.

This virus is exponentially contagious in places where many people live close to each other. It is taking a heavy toll in the densely populated working-class neighbourhoods of big cities, just as the Spanish flu, cholera, and the plague did in the past. This virus needs social contact. It finds this contact more readily in tower blocks where many people are living in close proximity, and in overcrowded neighbourhoods with little greenery and outdoor space. Very often it is the neighbourhoods where many front-line workers live that the virus is nurtured; day in and day out these workers also come into contact with many people in the course of their duties. 'Just like any other disease, COVID-19 has a strong socio-economic dimension. This dimension is territorially anchored,' concludes Parisian Professor Nadine Levratto from her research. British journalist Owen Jones doesn't mince his words: 'It goes without saying that the virus is a class issue.'

* * *

Sofie Merckx has been living for many years in Charleroi where she is a General Practitioner for the local centre of Medicine for the People. She is perfectly fluent in both Dutch and French, just like Raoul Hedebouw, our flamboyant parliamentary group leader. In her first year as a member of parliament, Sofie succeeded in making her mark. Political commentator Luc Van der Kelen calls her 'an asset to Belgian politics'.

Sofie has been instrumental in securing a place for patients' associations and a consultative voice within the committee for reimbursement of pharmaceuticals. With the crisis, she is making the voice of 'Medicine for the People' heard. In a debate with no less than five ministers in charge of protective mouth masks and an even greater number of health ministers, she is overcome with frustration: 'Say, do you really think all those people have forgotten all that right away, or what?' When Sofie Merckx gets angry, she uses the dialect of her native Antwerp, even in parliament.

At the end of June 2020, Dr. Sofie is laughing, satisfied: 'A big step forward! COVID-19 is recognised as an occupational disease.' Anyone who was working in a crucial sector or essential service during the lockdown and contracted the virus can have the condition recognised as an occupational disease, just as was previously the case for healthcare workers. With the Workers' Party of Belgium, we have been struggling for such recognition for two months. We have introduced a legislative proposal on the subject. To the workers, it makes a world of difference. Recognition as an occupational disease ensures full reimbursement of medical expenses and entitlement to ninety percent of one's basic salary. Whoever gets COVID-19 does not turn destitute right away as is the case in the United States. There, lots of people cannot afford healthcare unless they are willing to pay huge amounts of money for the rest of their lives. In such a scenario, you may recover from COVID-19, but you will never recover from the bills.

'We would have loved our scheme to apply to all workers, regardless of their area of activity. That is the objective for which we will keep striving,' says Sofie. 'In any case, the risk of contamination is greater in the workplace than anywhere else. We would also have liked to see more than just the one and a half metres rule of social distancing. In consultation with the trade unions, we have submitted a more comprehensive proposal that also takes into account contaminated objects, surfaces, and materials'.

* * *

'Non Siamo Carne da Macello'

'It is all a matter of balance.' This is how commentators describe it. 'A fine balance between [the] economy and health.' Indeed, but it is a balance the stability of which is subject to power relations. Nothing in life is free, after all. Except for the virus, and even in that respect we are not equal.

At the outbreak of the pandemic, many restrictions had to be imposed. In Spain, people were only allowed to leave the house for urgent errands or medical appointments. The police had the authority to check whether you had really been to a shop and to inspect your shopping bags or request your receipt. In France, you had to carry a written statement every time you left the house. Practicing sports was only allowed at certain times of the day. In Poland, the maximum distance you could walk your dog away from home was 1,200 metres; not one metre more. Taking a stroll in the park or in the forest was forbidden.

In Belgium, whole neighbourhoods were locked down, playgrounds cordoned off, cafes and restaurants closed, and theatres and sports facilities slammed shut. Gatherings were forbidden immediately and one measure more or less was of no concern. 'Stay at home! I really mean it!' one of our nine Health Ministers kept telling us. A song has actually been written on the subject: *Stay at home*! Such is our civic duty, except when it comes to big business. Then it gets much more complicated. Maybe you should not stay 'at home', after all as though workplaces were not gatherings. In order not to upset management, the word lockdown was not even supposed to be spoken here. 'Ceci n'est pas une pipe' (Magritte's famous painting of a pipe, named 'This is not a pipe'), we all know that. On Friday 13 March, when the first measures were taking effect, Minister-President Jan Jambon made the following statement on *De Ochtend Radio*: 'I wouldn't explicitly call it lockdown, but rather decisive measures.'

When the virus set foot on Italian soil, a bitter fight over COVID-19 broke out in the workplace: death through the virus on the one hand or economic damage through lockdown on the other hand. The one is measured against the other on the scale. A macabre balancing act between two realities. People's health, on the one hand, the market economy, which, by the way, was created by man, on the other hand. The mighty Confindustria (Confederazione Generale dell'Industria Italiana) padroni (bosses) did everything in their power to keep production running. They also got the support of the extreme right-wing, which – when all is said and done – will always support the great patronage.

The Italian TV series *Gomorrah*, titled after Roberto Saviano's bestseller, was sickening at times. The author is quite used to rabid injustice from the Italian mafia. But what he saw at the outbreak of the pandemic horrified him: 'In Italy, the strongest and wealthiest region was the least willing to deal with the pandemic. The leaders there have made choices for which they must account sooner or later. They have prevented workers from staying home. They have forced them to choose between their life and their job. This has been a contributing factor to this massive contamination, with an incredibly high death toll as a result. We are talking here about a region where the ruling class decided "not to be hindered". Where they were aware of the danger of a carnage and where they deliberately opted for a "gamble".'

Luca is employed in a metallurgical company that produces casings for whipped cream canisters, in the heavily affected region of Emilia-Romagna. The workshop's rotating machines make a hell of a noise. The only way colleagues could communicate was by getting close to each other. On those factory floors, shouting is the norm. In the event of a work-related death, the company contributes a thousand euros to the funeral costs. But Luca is wondering whether making whipped cream canisters is that necessary right now. 'Surely health is not to be quantified in monetary terms. Life is priceless.'

Yet, at the start of the pandemic, there was no intention whatsoever of sacrificing the slightest part of the economy 'to a flu that had gotten out of hand'. They were counting on 'herd' immunity. A certain number of people would die, of course. But that would happen quickly, and the economic impact would be less damaging. Only when it became clear that the public would not tolerate the huge mortality rate in the overburdened Lombardy hospitals, when the protests of the medical staff against the inhumane triage became louder and louder, and when it was already far too late to avoid needless mortality, only then did they close a part of the economy for a while.

Despite the rising death toll, the lobbying groups of large companies kept trying to keep their sectors open. The US Embassy in Italy was moving heaven and earth to keep the Leonard factories in Cameri, Italy open in the very midst of the lockdown. According to them, assembling F-35 fighter planes was essential, at a time when the number of those infected and deaths were skyrocketing. Elsewhere, car lobbies were sticking out their tentacles to ensure that the production of cars be considered an essential human activity.

On Monday 13 April I got an email from Greta: 'Dear Peter, my son is employed at the Honda storage facility. They already had to send people home because they were coughing. But my son has to carry on working. I am scared stiff.' On the same evening, Minister-President Jan Jambon came on VTM news with the following statement: 'We are all in the same boat. There is no contradiction between a sound economy and good health.' What would Greta make of this? In Belgium, contradictions are simply disposed of, even on live television. That type of magic makes Houdini look like small fry. After pulling his stunt, the Minister-President was driven back to his villa in Brasschaat by his driver, in the official car, of course. Do you really believe Greta's son was sitting with him in the same boat?

* * *

In quite a few sectors, it was the workers themselves who were pressing the pause button on production. 'Non siamo carne da macello.' We are not cannon fodder. It was under this banner that tens of thousands of Italian workers went on strike. Francesca Re David, head of the Italian Metalworkers, had been invited to the Worker's Party of Belgium's digital 1-May celebration. This is what she told us: 'The metal workers were the first to make a decision: stop production with unsafe working conditions. The mandatory measures taken against COVID-19 outside the factory should also be taken inside the factory, i.e., guarantee a distance of at least one and a half metres and provide sufficient protective material for each member of the workforce. We went on strike in order to ensure our safety. First, we struck at a local level, for example, at the Fiat plant. After that we struck at a national level. We struck until Confindustria gave in and signed a protocol. Only then did the government intervene. It finally decided to bring all non-essential businesses to a standstill. We, however, had to fight for those protocols first.'

Under pressure from the labour movement, non-essential businesses closed, and part of the economy came to a standstill. In Belgium, the Brussels Audi workers, the Ghent Volvo Truck workers, and the Liège Safran Aero Booster workers compelled the management to suspend production temporarily. In France, Amazon France was served a court order prohibiting it from shipping products other than essential products. The court ruled that the company must involve the trade unions in the analysis of occupational risks in the workplace.

No sooner had the process to institute the measures begun, a battle began to have them removed. In *The New York Times*, conservative chroniclers, among them Thomas Friedman, immediately started a campaign against the lockdown regulations. 'They are useless because you cannot win the battle against Mother Nature', they said. 'We have to see to it that the cure does not make things worse than the disease itself.'

People were hearing exactly the same mantra in Germany. 'Your money or your life', the *Frankfurter Allgemeine Zeitung* headlined a mere four days after the introduction of social distancing. The newspaper was annoyed about the fact that 'the government is now mainly following the virologists' advice'. Just imagine allowing science to outweigh economics! The newspaper concluded: 'Both President Donald Trump and Alexander Dibelius, the former manager of Goldman Sachs, have made it clear in recent days that they consider the price of the protective measures to be too high. The cure has now become worse than the disease; this is also Trump's understanding.'

'We have to see to it that the cure does not make things worse than the disease itself.' President Trump repeated this sentence ad nauseam. In Flanders, Bart De Wever, the leader of the New Flemish Alliance (N-VA) played copycat with the very same sentence. N-VA Member of Parliament Koen Metsu submitted a plan to get everyone under the age of sixty back to work. 'It is inevitable that some people will get infected while we are waiting for a vaccine,' says Metsu. The 'some people' he was talking about are precisely the workers who had to go back to work. He did not say a word about protective measures for these workers.

Throughout the month of April, Belgian Prime Minister Wilmès and Flanders' Minister-President Jambon kept repeating over and over the same words: resume, restart, relaunch; 'It is a fact, the country needs to start over'. But in which direction is this restart? Not to ask this question is in itself an answer: We need to get back to business as usual as quickly as possible. 'If the mortality rate drops, perhaps we should say: so what?' That's what the CEO of a large plastics company told the business newspaper *De Tijd*. Some collateral damage happens at the workplace? So what? The heroes must work and keep silent.

* * *

When the companies finally resumed operations, the trade unions helped to enforce safety measures on the shop floor. The

'Safe at Work' guide contains excellent measures to provide a safe working environment and to make the necessary arrangements: unfortunately, it is 'not mandatory'. And thus, a new chapter has been opened everywhere in the struggle for respect of the health rules in the workplace.

In Detroit, the Chrysler workers demanded a ten-minute break every hour to ventilate the workshops. They insisted on being able to keep sufficient distance between workers both during the change of shifts and in the canteen. Above all, they insisted that workers are entitled to object to working conditions, which they deem unsafe. This is important. It is important that people be allowed to assess by themselves whether the environment is safe or not. This cannot possibly be assessed by a manager sitting in front of his computer. They are right. As workers are making their voices heard, the necessary sanitary measures are put in place and this helps. You will see one constant everywhere: the firmer the union stands, the safer the workplace gets.

The Invisibles

'Dockworker (50) Bakes Chips and Gives Them Away for Free to Thank Healthcare Staff.' Antwerp dockworker, Jurgen, treats the staff from healthcare centres to free chips from his mobile French-Fry truck Don Patat. 'To promote the Belgian chips, our national pride, on the one hand. And also, to encourage and support the healthcare personnel. A portion of free chips to thank them is the least we can do. We, dockworkers, sometimes hit the headlines for negative reasons. But, as you can see, we are far from being that bad', he chuckles with a broad smile. I have posted the message on Facebook along with a big red heart. On the picture, alongside the article, are three nurses eating chips in front of Jurgen's stall. Two nurses in the picture are black. Lots of 'likes' have been added to the post, but also, some racist remarks against 'black people'.

Before the outbreak of the crisis, healthcare personnel in Belgium were invisible. They were, however, there and we knew it. But nobody would notice their presence. Nobody wanted to see them. Almost one out of six healthcare providers in our country are of foreign origin. In the various 'essential services' as a whole, one out of five workers is an immigrant. At 8 p.m. we would clap at our front doors for one minute; twelve seconds of each minute were devoted to the heroes of a different origin. In our country, one fifth of the workers employed in the food sector, the waste-disposal sector, as well as in public transport, are of non-Belgian origin. Our heroes are diverse. This is also true in Germany, Sweden, Austria, and Italy: one in five 'essential workers' is an immigrant. They are mainly employed in the cleaning, healthcare, and food sectors.

* * *

By the end of June, even before there was any indication of a second wave, new clusters began appearing in Europe: in Spain, Italy, England, and Germany. In our country, Belgium, there was a lot of speculation about travel warnings and quarantine for vacationers returning from affected areas. The fact that these clusters were appearing in places where working and living conditions are miserable escaped attention – places in Europe where modern slavery is rampant.

In the draughty cellars of British Leicester, for instance, migrant workers assemble pieces of fabric for less than four euros per hour in one of the hundreds of sewing workshops where ten thousand people are crammed together and working like slaves, often in appalling conditions. Where subcontractors ignored the lockdown and forced sick workers to come to work under penalty of dismissal. Where, meanwhile, the parent company, the fast-fashion internet chain Boohoo, washed its hands of any responsibility.

The same conditions exist in the drab annex buildings of the Italian Viadana, on the plain of the Po river, where hundreds of workers are huddled together in slaughterhouses and meat-processing plants. It is equally true for agricultural workers who are packed together like animals in the stench of mosquito-filled stables without light or running water, as is the case in the Catalan town of Aitona near Lleida, where thousands and thousands of peach trees are waiting to be picked.

They number in the millions, the invisible people working themselves to exhaustion day after day after day. They work in residential barracks, ready-to-wear sewing factories, in fields as well as on construction sites. Their resilience is reduced. The measures for social distancing are not applied. They are packed in like sardines in the minivans that carry them to and from the workplace or huddled on their mattresses in the sleeping areas. Such are the bleak conditions that are fueling this new pandemic. Class-defined environments nobody is talking about, except when the virus threatens to spread and spill over into other areas of society.

'This virus has forced our society to take a look in the mirror. It has exposed society's inequalities and injustices. We all knew they were there, but we had turned our backs on them. We ought to use the memory of this pandemic as an incentive to search for truth.' In the words of Richard Horton, editor-in-chief of the authoritative medical journal *The Lancet*. 'The truth is most of the tens of thousands of deaths could have been prevented. This a dreadful wound we should not ignore.'

* * *

One Saturday in June 2020, a heavily pregnant woman went to the hospital in Sessa Aurunca, about fifty kilometres north of Naples, to give birth. The baby boy she delivered was healthy and well. Yet the woman tested positive for COVD-19, though she was showing no symptoms. She is a farmhand from Bulgaria. She is employed as a tomato picker and lives in one of the five dilapidated eleven-story apartment buildings standing in the Cirio district of the nearby coastal town of Mondragone. These buildings serve as sleeping places, 'dormitories', for 700 seasonal workers, people from Bulgaria, Romania, Poland, and Moldavia. On that same Saturday, a man from her district also tested positive at the Sessa Aurunca hospital. Warning bells started ringing. A complete lockdown of the district was ordered. Everybody was tested. Forty-three people tested positive.

These were seasonal workers who, at the beginning of the harvest season, had come to work in the tomato, green bean, and melon fields of the hills surrounding Mondragone. Most of them were from Bulgaria. No one else would be willing to spend the whole day bending down under the blazing sun for a pittance. 'The entire agricultural sector in this province of Caserta is dependent on foreign workers for its operations,' trade unionist Tammaro Della Corte stated. 'They can work twelve-hour days in the fields for a wage of thirty to forty euros a day, the women for even less. Of that, five euros is paid to their intermediary employer. Even the price of a drink or a mid-day sandwich is deducted from their pay. The contractors pick them up at four o'clock in the morning at the roundabouts and drive them to the countryside. It is not unusual to have sixteen people crammed in a van with a nine-passenger capacity, even in the midst of the crisis.'

These farmhands are there to ensure that the tomatoes, green beans, and melons they pick reach our tables. They are at the very bottom of the food chain, forgotten heroes in forgotten fields. When they stand up for their rights, the extreme right-wing is very quick to sow dissent. 'The virus has been brought by the Roma people of Bulgaria' is the call posted on social media by the far right-wing about those of Mondragone. Matteo Salvini of the right-wing extremist party the Lega went there to provoke Italians and, in the words of Roberto Saviano 'to spew his scorn about the guest workers who are staying there'. The extreme right-wing did not say a single word about the living and working conditions of these modern-day slaves. 'The foreigners' are the ones to blame for the virus. This is how they succeed in playing off one part of the working class against the other. In the meantime, major landowners and agricultural companies are rubbing their hands together with glee.

* * *

One thousand six hundred and fifty-six kilometres north in Gütersloh, in the German state of North Rhine-Westphalia, one could hear the same thing: 'The virus comes from Bulgaria'. This is where the Tönnies Fleisch slaughterhouse, the biggest in Europe, is located. With its seven thousand workers, it has the capacity to process as many as 30,000 pigs per day! Discount giants such as Lidl and Aldi impose 'dumping' prices in order to keep their schnitzels cheap, but above all to make excessive profits. Meanwhile, their owners have become billionaires, among them Mr. Tönnies, the pig magnate, valued at 2 billion euros. The farmer at the start of the chain is a victim. He has two choices: lose his business or participate in the industrial mass production of meat.

Mid-June 2020, four-fifths of the workers of the Tönnies Fleisch plant tested positive. Most of them come from Romania and Bulgaria. 'At this hellish pace, you can hardly expect rules of social distancing or hygiene to be respected,' says a man from the food workers' union. The workers at Tönnies' work a six-day week, in eleven-hour shifts, for puny minimum wages. They are not officially employed by Tönnies. They work as 'independent subcontractors' for other 'middlemen' subcontractors who have recruited them in Poland, Romania or Bulgaria and with whom they have signed work contracts. Almost all of the 7,000 workers at Tönnies are working for twenty-five of these subcontractors. A cascade of companies linked to the slaughterhouse.

Their contracts often include a rental clause. This clause is not a gift, however. For a paltry bunk bed in overcrowded barrack-type buildings, huge amounts of money are deducted from their wages. These conditions make them even more vulnerable. If they speak out, they also risk losing their shelter. Unexpected overtime hours are numerous at Tönnies', as are unpaid working hours. Trade unionists are being threatened and work-related accidents are reclassified by Romanian doctors into 'non-work-related' accidents. The health of a 'subcontractor' will usually deteriorate after a few years; the middlemen subcontractors easily replace the one for another.

The fact that slaughterhouses are places where hundreds of people got infected is no coincidence. The European Union's accolades for the 'supreme form of freedom', the free movement of workers across European borders, means, in the real world, that armies of Bulgarians, Romanians, and Poles are living like slaves. Exploited and exhausted, they commute between the workplace and their slave quarters. In this real world, occupational safety is non-existent and works' councils and prevention committees are the exception. Is it any wonder then, that the virus should proliferate there?

The shameless pursuit of profit by meat baron Tönnies forced the entire neighbourhood into lockdown for a second time in just a few months. Businesses closed down. Schools closed. Shops closed. Residential blocks closed. Tens of thousands of people were deprived of their freedom of movement and their sources of income. But the word shame is something our pig magnate doesn't know. Billionaire Tönnies asked for state assistance. According to him, the government must compensate him for the economic repercussions from the unemployment of his factory workers. His slaughter paradise must be reopened without delay. Clemens Tönnies finances; Clemens Tönnies donates; and Clemens Tönnies dictates.

Tönnies has connections in practically all political parties and meets with these political leaders in beautiful leather armchairs. The shiny black armchairs are in the lodges of his football club, Schalke 04. As a secondary occupation, he has been chairman of the club for many years. This is where he is used to meeting people like Armin Laschet, the conservative prime minister of North Rhine-Westphalia. When COVID-19 broke out, Laschet said that the virus had probably returned 'from Bulgaria'. The Bulgarian virus! This national chauvinism is how people get pitted against one another in factories, which is a good thing for the meat tycoon sitting at the top.

On Twitter, there was a great deal of anger: 'That company should have given up such nauseating labour practices long ago.' Even the Schalke supporters were fed up. On 29 June, they formed a long human chain with banners and protest signs all around the football club's fields. President Clemens Tönnies, who was already the subject of criticism for his chauvinistic statements, had to leave. On the very next day he stepped down from his role as chairman.

'That Mr. Tönnies and Mr. Laschet are now blaming the guest workers is despicable. The terrible conditions in German slaughterhouses have been known for many years.' Sahra Wagenknecht is angry. She is a delegate for Die Linke in the German Bundestag. 'For twenty years, the federal authorities have organized wage dumping, work contracts, and out-sourcing to subcontractors,' she said. 'As a result, we have German slaughterhouses where workers are hardly treated any better than the cattle they have to process.' In spite of all the attempts made by the extreme right to hijack the debate and divert it to nationalist issues, the discussions in Germany are about working conditions and social injustice. This is not only essential, but it also brings hope.

* * *

One hundred and seventy-five years ago, Friedrich Engels wrote the bestseller titled 'The Condition of the Working Class in England'. He was twenty-four years-old. In his book, the young author made a link between living and working conditions on the one hand and health on the other hand. Engels is one of the first ever to apply the working methods of epidemiologists, charting data accurately.

Disease is not the cause of material deprivation. It is a contributing factor, of course, but material deprivation does prompt the massive spread of disease, Engels explains. Injuries, accidents at work, deaths in the workplace – so long as it is only the lower class that is affected – are not such a big problem. For every dead worker, there will be two new ones beating down the door to get his job.

With epidemics, however, things are different, because epidemics also threaten the richer neighbourhoods. 'When the epidemic was approaching, a universal terror seized the bourgeoisie of the city of Manchester. People remembered the unwholesome dwellings of the poor, and trembled before the certainty that each of these slums would become a centre for the plague, whence it would spread desolation in all directions through the houses of the propertied class'. Friedrich Engels continues: 'A Health Commission was appointed at once to investigate these districts, and report upon their condition to the Town Council.'

What were the results of this commission? 'There were inspected, in all, 6,951 houses. Of these, 2,565 urgently needed whitewashing within; 960 were out of repair; 959 had insufficient drains; 1,455 were damp; 452 were badly ventilated; 2,221 were without privies.' The situation was such that action had to be taken. Engels continues: 'To cleanse such an Augean stable before the arrival of the cholera was, of course, out of the question. A few of the worst nooks were therefore cleansed, and everything else left as before. In the cleansed spots the old filthy condition was naturally restored in a couple of months.'

Today, we no longer see twelve to sixteen Irish or Scottish textile workers living together in damp English workers' slums. The situation has changed, but not significantly. Today, a cheap thirty-square meter flat will accommodate as many as six to eight workers from Eastern Europe. Today, they do not spend sixteen hours each day toiling in noisy textile factories anymore. Instead, they work thirteen-hour days in huge butcheries and vast fruit fields. The massive spread of COVID-19 in such situations was as predictable as it was when cholera broke out in nineteenth-century Manchester and as it is now with the furious surge of the virus in the São Paolo favelas, where the extreme right-wing president, Jair Bolsonaro, is doing everything he can to ignore the ravages of the disease.

The Sleeping Giant is Awake

COVID-19 has awakened Sleeping Beauty with a smacker! A sleeping giant has come back to life: the working class. It was impressive to see how much money was being poured into healthcare last summer. In France, in Germany, and in Belgium, we are talking about millions of euros. Behind all that money lies fear. Fear that this white anger can no longer be controlled; that people have arisen who could inspire others.

The rise of the white anger worldwide could quicken the pace of a wider movement. This is the movement of a working class that is regaining its pride, a self-awareness of the essential workers. An invisible class that has stepped out of its own shadow and will not let itself be pushed back into darkness.

'Florence Nightingale is not working here anymore.' These words were written on a banner carried by American nurses. In the US, Florence Nightingale is known as the primeval mother of nurses, the symbol of the submissive nurse who is always on standby and never bangs her fist on the table. Today, Nightingale has been discarded, not the cheerful and committed Florence, only her slavish and meek alter ego. This also is happening in Belgium. For centuries, the healthcare sector has been controlled by charities. Only recently, in the late 1980s, did the white anger rise. It has matured during COVID-19, all over the world. A proud group of caregivers is growing who appreciate being cheered, but more importantly, who pursue their rights. White coats who know to command respect.

This is also happening in the maintenance sector. Our society has a long tradition of disdain and contempt for domestic workers and cleaning teams. They are ordered around like servants. People look down on them with disdain. They are underpaid; in Europe they often earn less than fourteen euros per hour. They are ignored. The arrival of the virus, however, has changed all that. Suddenly, hygiene has become vitally important.

The people in charge of cleaning our homes, our residential care centres, our hospitals, and our buildings, had already left for Brussels just before the outbreak of the pandemic to demand a decent minimum wage that was arrogantly refused them by the big cleaning companies. Today, they are back.

The crisis has put working people in the forefront of the battle against the pandemic and the economic devastation because of what they do. Until now, they have always been seen as abstract cost items on a balance sheet, mere data meant to carry out 'their duties' as well as possible. Just how much society depends on their work has become clear today. They are now visible: caretakers, shelf fillers, garbage collectors, dockworkers, logistics staff, parcel-delivery staff, shop assistants, van drivers, farm workers, meat processors, you name it. The Genie is released from Aladdin's magical lamp now and he must not re-enter the lamp of silent passivity. It is not the stock markets that have kept things running; nor is it the stock exchange making the world go round; and the chattering class certainly doesn't know the meaning of real work. We, the working class, did it. We are the ones who made sure that society continued to function.

A new dynamic force has emerged from below, from the work floor. In many workplaces, employees have joined together and taken action, often for the first time in their lives. To them, the safeguarding of fundamental rights – health, safety, life itself – was worth a major effort. They are stirring. They are uniting, formulating demands, obtaining results, and regaining a sense of pride. At times, they have fallen flat on their faces, of course, suffered defeats, and taken some hard knocks. In the darkest of times, they have, however, risen again.

'Employers want to go back to business as usual.' The tide has turned, however. Caregivers, workers in the healthcare industry, in supermarkets, and in transport have now become the real heroes. This is a fact. They have kept the country afloat and now they want decent jobs. They are finished with zero-hour contracts, fake statutes, and precarious work. Tony Burke is a trade unionist in his heart and his soul. He watches as confidence in the trade unions is skyrocketing in Great Britain. Since the start of the pandemic, the number of union members has risen by more than 100,000. The number of women joining is remarkable; never before seen in the last quarter of the past century have so many women become members of the British trade unions. The trade unions have also stood up together with the working classes.

Most of the traditional politicians have been targeting the trade unions over the past decades. The trade unions did not get involved in big media or in political debates. For years the media and the politicians collectively bashed the unions. Not one good word could be heard about the defenders of the working class. Now, however, it appears that the virus has brought the unions back to life. While confidence in the government was dwindling day after day, confidence in the trade unions was growing. While we were sinking into the darkness of the crisis, thousands of trade unionists were doing everything they could to ensure financial relief was paid to millions of people and answers were given to the innumerable questions raised about the jumbled measures taken at various levels of government. These trade unionists have proposed support measures, secured benefits, and denounced and banned arbitrariness such as 'free dismissal during temporary unemployment'. In many places, they have helped to protect jobs and to enforce safe working conditions on the job.

'It is a matter of democracy,' says Tony Burke. 'The working class has tackled the crisis. Too many workers have died. We are paying the price for this crisis right now. Why should we restore the old order? The world has changed. The working people have vindicated their claim to a place in society. They must be given a real say in strong unions. This is the key for the recession that is now on its way as well.'

A member of the General Labor Federation of Belgium (FGTB), Arnaud Levêque, joins in: 'If the unions succeed in creating a collective consciousness, then an awful lot is possible. A new class consciousness can lead to a reversal in the balance of power. This balance has been to our disadvantage for the past forty years due to the rise of neoliberalism. That period saw a slow but steady decline in the willingness of the trade unions to fight for social change. The pandemic has brought a brutal change of context. A whole range of possibilities is now emerging. But then we must be well aware of our collective weight.'

The first thing heroes need to realize is that they are heroes. While politicians were turning it all into a shameful mess, ordinary people pulled out all the stops in order to keep the country afloat. They have been doing that for a long time, but this is the first time it was acknowledged. The self-confidence gained by the producing class is the essential ingredient of change.

It is but normal that we should applaud the working class and not those who give orders, chatter, and speculate. Cheers are not enough, though. It is unacceptable that the very people who saved the country should have to take the blows again tomorrow – in their jobs, their income, and their health. It is unacceptable that the lies of the past should be served up again tomorrow. It is abhorrent that there should be no money for healthcare or for a decent life for our seniors; that there should be no money to get people out of poverty. It is repugnant that it is impossible to redistribute the perversely accumulated wealth at the top of society; that there should be no time for family and relatives; and that everyone should work like hell seven days a week. It is unacceptable that society's motto remains 'every man for himself'; that collectivity no longer exists in any form.

The old way of thinking is being swept away. Let us make sure no one picks it up and reheats it in the microwave oven. This is a matter of hygiene!

Today, the working class has the authority to act. It has succeeded in keeping the country upright during the most difficult period.

They Have Forgotten Us

PART II

Care

> I refer to Bertolt Brecht who, in his play *Life of Galilei*,
> asked the question, 'What is the purpose of science?'
> He gave the following answer: 'Not to open the doors to eternal wisdom,
> but to close them to ignorance.'
> When democracy works, it allows reason to have a voice.
> Giuseppe Ippolito, Director of the Spallanzani Institute

Friday 17 April 2020, the virus is wreaking havoc. The obituaries in the newspapers were taking up three times more space than usual. Marianne Zwagerman tweets: 'Emotion definitely has to be removed from the debate. The dry wood is felled, perhaps a few months earlier than without the virus. Should all those who are still in the prime of life sacrifice everything for that?' Zwagerman is a writer and opinion maker at the Dutch newspaper *De Telegraaf*.

That is really what she said. Emotion must be eliminated from the debate. The dry wood has to be cut. That declaration drove a stake through the heart of so many people. Reactions were immediate: 'Does this mean that my parents, who are in their 70s, do not deserve a fulfilling retirement? What about my Dad with the two new knees he had to receive due to a life of hard work in construction, would you call him dry wood? What about me: in an at-risk group, no spleen, forty-six years old, always at work? Should I also drop dead?' Zwagerman was quiet.

Everywhere one finds heartless and self-serving people who dare to wonder out loud whether 'all of this' is worth it. 'All of this' means the 'sacrifice' of 'healthy young forces', a society at a standstill, and 'the pause button for the economy'. All of this for a group of people who have had their share of life and are going to die anyway, albeit a few months earlier than normal. That is what the cold-blooded said. They forgot that we are all dying as soon as we are born. They forgot that we are all born again every day to embrace life, even at the age of ninety-four.

Do you really have to feel ashamed of being part of the community once you have reached a certain age? Simone de Beauvoir tackled this issue in 'La Vieillesse' (Old Age). Older people have the same desires, the same feelings, and the same demands as young people. They are exactly that – people. The image of the venerable, wise, and silent elderly is a cultural construction. The same holds true for its counter-image of the stammering and demented old person. De Beauvoir marvels at the ease with which abuse, scandal, and drama are accepted when it comes to the elderly. Eventually, she argues, the cultural level of a community can be assessed from the way it treats its elderly.

Apparently, this level is not very high. This is exemplified by the implicit banishment of ageing people from the community.

It is also said that elderly people are 'a problem'; a social problem and in this context, they are a numerical problem. It takes 'painful measures' to cope with demographic ageing. In other words, each one of the elderly should count her/himself lucky and be grateful for what the community is doing for her or him. As if these now elderly people had not been spending their whole lives shaping the community and thus bringing their contributions to it.

The gatekeepers of the status quo have no qualms about asking what a human life is 'worth'. To them, this is not a philosophical matter, but clearly only an economic issue. Human beings turned into figures on the macabre profit-based balance sheets. All that lives is reduced to profitability and the 'unprofitable' are subsequently forced to give way. *Prolonged illness? Unprofitable! A handicap? Unprofitable! Too old? Unprofitable! Away with the unprofitable! Away with emotion! Long live economics! Let's cut it down, that dry wood!*

Care

French philosopher Edgar Morin scornfully declares: 'Economic logic, [in today's society] is more important and is stronger than human logic'. Aged 99, Morin has been around for almost a century. He reflects: 'Profit is worth much more to them than the loss of individuals due to the epidemic. After all, sacrificing the most fragile, the elderly, and the sick, has a function in the natural-selection logic. In the business world, those who are not capable of withstanding competition are bound to perish. If we want an authentic human society, we must oppose this social Darwinism at all costs.'

Giving everyone a chance to have a decent life in their older days, this is truly human. Which choice are we going to make? What type of society do we want? The elderly in the community are not necessarily the last. They are the first. They are the discoverers, the pioneers, those who have taught us everything, those who came before us. The elderly are not the past. They are the future. They are at a point in life that we still have to reach.

* * *

'At Times, as Many as Three Hearses Would Leave Here in One Single Day'

Fourteen years ago, in 2006, a group of Belgian academics drew up a roadmap for the control of infectious diseases in residential care centres at the request of the federal government. That roadmap was tested in an extensive pilot project. What was the result? Excellent! What about the price? Hardly anything! For an average of 20,000 euros, a residential care centre could be ready at all times to respond adequately to an outbreak. Compared to the millions of euros swallowed up by big business in that sector in recent years, it is peanuts. A fraction of that big money could have covered the cost of an adequate supply of masks, alcohol-based sanitizer gel, and protective aprons as well as the cost of training additional staff and could have contributed to the development of an effective collaboration between neighbouring hospitals.

None of that happened. The roadmap was simply binned. When residential care in Belgium became a regional matter in 2014, infectious disease control disappeared into the black hole of regionalisation. No one has seen the roadmap since. We have paid a big price for that in this crisis.

Over a period of three months, almost five thousand people died of COVID-19 in residential care centres. We should also add to this list the residents of care centres who died in the hospital. Probably two out of three fatalities in Belgium are residents of a care centre. The retirement homes are our own Lombardy.

On 1 March, the spring break (a week-long school holiday) was coming to an end and the skiers were returning home. In two East Flemish residential care centres an employee came back infected. The centres were faced with an outbreak of the virus at a very early stage of the pandemic. At that point, masks were the only thing that could have helped. We can understand that they did not want to impose an obligation on the entire sector. They were in short supply. But why should the use of masks be discouraged in residential care centres that did have them in stock? This is something we could not understand This is how more residents got infected and the death toll grew.

The shortage of masks was not the only issue at stake. The boat began sinking. Things were spinning out of control; it was chaotic. There was also a clear lack of decisiveness. When the retirement homes locked down on 12 March, we were made to understand that the virus would not enter them. Yet the virus did enter, and what's more, it came in through the front door. Eighty-year-old people were isolated from their children and grand-children; they were hurriedly introduced to the techniques of video calls; and birthday balloons were released in front of their windows. Meanwhile, the virus was simply ushered in on the shoulders of the staff.

'We don't have enough soap. Soap! Let alone hydro-alcoholic gel!' The day after the lockdown was imposed, a union representative for residential care centres sounded the alarm: 'We don't have anything: no gloves, no aprons, no goggles, no gel!'

Healthcare workers were asked to avoid 'waste' and to wear their masks for eight hours, 'regardless of the sequence of interventions'. In the meantime, care personnel could hear on the radio and TV that masks retained their effectiveness for a maximum of four hours. There was an ominously huge gap between what serious people were saying as to what should be done and the situation on the ground. Panic was growing. The politicians were using soothing words to say that the situation would be brought under control soon. We now know that wasn't the case. The problem didn't get resolved. Dirk Snauwaert, the Director of a Residential Care Centre in Bruges, summed things up: 'It was war. I had to send my people to the front. But we didn't have any bullets. Initially, hospitals were at the centre of attention. It was considered that residential care centres were places where one goes to die anyway and that if they pass away a bit sooner than expected, that's the way it is.'

It is noteworthy that on 25 March, the experts, including Professor Erika Vlieghe, expert in Infectious Diseases and Tropical Medicine at the University Hospital Antwerp, proposed to take over and coordinate the strategy for residential care centres at a federal level. It was a sensible offer. The situation on the ground was crying out for a centralised approach and, at that time, nobody had the slightest idea of what the situation was like in the residential care centres of Belgium. Flanders, however refused. 'This falls under our competence', was the Jambon government's position, as if the virus cared about language or competence. The virus is flexible and easily adapts; the same cannot be said about the authorities in Belgium. It took the Flemish side another two long weeks to set up a plan and organize a task force for healthcare that were finally submitted by Minister Beke on 8 April 2020.

Such fragmentation kills any efficiency. In mid-July, Erika Vlieghe testified in the Flemish Parliament: 'Responsibility does not lie with one structure only or one minister alone'. 'The issue of unity at [the] command level is very real. And it is cause for great concern. '

From early April onwards, not a day went by without promises being made that the personnel of retirement homes would be tested. *Paroles, paroles* (words), Dalida used to sing. Everybody was competent, nobody was responsible. The regional ministers shifted responsibility to the federal authority who would immediately pass the buck back. Like Pontius Pilate, the ministers washed their hands in innocence while the unrest was growing in the healthcare sector.

'As sick residents were being tested, a nurse approached me. Would I please test her as well? Her husband was sitting at home with a chronic disease, and she was scared to death at the idea that she could take the virus home. She was ready to stay overnight for the next few weeks at the workplace if she tested positive', Dr. Lise Vandecasteele told me. That was 4 April, 2020. Politicians and the media were focusing on the hospitals while the drama was taking place in residential care centres. In those days, sixty people would die every day in the Flemish residential care centres; and that was before the peak came on Easter weekend. While the curve was subsiding elsewhere, it sky-rocketed in the retirement homes. 'At times, as many as three hearses would leave here in one single day', Director Snauwaert testified.

One thing is certain, everyone on the ground was doing their level best. Health professionals, doctors, kitchen staff, cleaning assistants, management, and volunteers were showing an almost inexhaustible motivation to fight the virus. There was anger; there was sadness; there was despair, incomprehension, and chaos; but everybody was working very hard. Everyone was mobilized. This solidarity carried the teams through the crisis. Help was coming from the Red Cross and other Non-Governmental Organizations (NGOs). More often than not, however, they were fighting a losing battle. The regional authorities finally gave the green light for testing the first residential care centres. Minister De Backer's task force testing team however, had provided the wrong manual: the swabs introduced into residents' noses were too thick and induced nosebleeds. Unskilled healthcare professionals did not see that the swabs they were using were throat swabs and not nose swabs. The procedure had to be started all over again. Teams from both Médecins Sans Frontières (Doctors Without Borders, usually sent on missions in war zones) and the army were hastily called in to help with testing.

As the government continued to stall and falter, a team from Medicine for the People was sent to the Zelzate Zilverbos retirement home on 7 April. Every resident as well as the staff were tested. This logistical, medical, and technical experience was accurately recorded in protocols and converted into a roadmap. Subsequently, mobile teams from Medicine for the People also tested retirement homes in Charleroi, Borsbeek, and Brussels. Yet when Dr. Sofie Merckx came to Parliament and presented this roadmap, which had been developed from this hands-on experience, as a concrete recommendation for use elsewhere, ministers De Backer and De Block looked away and never even responded.

Left to Fend for Themselves was the title of the report made by the doctors from Médecins Sans Frontières regarding the interventions they carried out in 135 residential care centres in early July. The words are harsh. The main conclusion: 'It is a fact that negligence has led to unnecessary deaths.'

'Negligence. Preventable deaths. Fact.' This should surely leave one speechless. On top of that, the report stated that 'We are not ready [for] another crisis of this magnitude'.

Flemish Minister-President Jan Jambon who, according to the Flemish newspaper *De Standaard* was 'totally absent in this crisis', has already made his own assessment. He is looking back, satisfied. 'Broadly speaking, we have done a good job. Looking at things in retrospect, one can always say: yes, but this or yes but that. It is always easier in hindsight. At the time, though, you have to make decisions. I don't think any mistakes were made that caused additional deaths.'

During the crisis, too many generals were tripping over each other's feet. Later on, however, they made shirking their responsibilities a wholesale business; they never made any mistakes.

'As a doctor and an MP, I was first in line to follow the Corona crisis. I took part in the work at the triage stations. I lost patients. Anxious nurses and desperate care home directors contacted me by phone,' said Dr. Lise Vandecasteele. Lise is one of the most active members of the Ad Hoc Committee on the COVID-19 Policy in the Flemish Parliament. 'Week after week, as I was standing in the middle of human tragedies and hearing the cries of distress, I would hear the soothing words Minister Beke was uttering from the domed hall of the Flemish Parliament. They were, in fact, long monologues aimed at giving the impression that everything was under control, when in the meantime a disaster was unfolding in the retirement homes. Week after week, the Flemish government was lagging behind events and the mortality rate was escalating. Week after week it was too little, too late.'

The Silver Market

Belgium has three systems for the care of senior citizens: the public system, usually managed by local authorities, the non-profit system, managed by non-profit organizations, and the commercial system, a booming market in the hands of large multinationals.

'Graailand' ('The Land of the Greedy'), my previous book, contains a chapter about the residential care centres. The book exposes many of the callous practices of these commercial groups such as spending barely three euros a day on meals for their residents; guidelines that provide replacement of nappies only when the saturation point has reached sixty-five percent; and the rules dictating that residents are provided a maximum of 130 to 150 grams of cooked vegetables a day and a maximum of 10 centilitres of meat gravy. Everything is measured and weighed so that every euro can be squeezed from the fees paid by the elderly.

Health care should not be privatized. The European Union however, refuses to ban private industry from operating within the health care system, especially for the care of the elderly. This opens the door for major players, very big players. Their private management rules apply only to their own centres, but there is a risk that they could become the norm in other centres as well. This is a shift from care-oriented thinking to market-oriented thinking.

It is not just a question of gravy and nappies, however. Nor is it just the operation of nursing homes. Rather it is the entire grouping of industries – property development, construction, maintenance and repair, and real estate management that generates millions of euros for its corporations.

The senior housing industry is now called the 'silver economy'. Local family businesses active in this silver market are gobbled up by international giants. In Flanders, the Senior Living Group, a branch of the French multinational Korian, has a stronghold on the sector, along with Armonea, founded by the richest families in Belgium – the Van den Brande family and the de Mévius of the brewery AB InBev. In early 2019, Armonea was taken over by the French giant Colisée. It currently has 270 rest homes in Europe and employs 18,000 people. Colisée's profit margin amounts to fifteen percent. Fifteen percent!

'The merry-go-round is spinning thanks to the money from the elderly who are faced with increasingly higher daily rates, and the money from the government that provides the necessary subsidies to pay for both staff and care' said Kris Cuyvers, an investment banker, who is sitting in the front row. The elder care commercial sector is, indeed, the goose that lays the golden eggs – or, in this case, rather 'silver' eggs.

Big commercial companies set up their own non-profit organizations that, in turn, operate their residential care centres. Why do they do this? Because they can receive government subsidies through these non-profit organizations, when, as commercial players, they are not eligible for them. These are therefore fictitious non-profit organizations that transfer millions of euros every month to their corporate patrons. They make these millions by charging exorbitant rents for their healthcare properties, much higher than anywhere else in the real estate industry. They also profit through charging 'vague' management fees. 'Over the past fifteen years, the focus has not been on welfare, but rather on growth and moneymaking – huge amounts of money.' Banker Cuyvers continues his blunt assessment: 'While care personnel – the white rage – were protesting in the streets of Brussels, real estate funds were rushing headlong into the lucrative side of the elderly-care market.'

The government's money is flowing not into better care for the elderly, but, via care-related real estate corporations, into the stock exchange. In the meantime, the healthcare providers toiling in a frantic race against time are fewer than ever before. In our neighbouring EU countries, there are eight care givers for everyone one hundred senior citizens; in Belgium we do not even have five.

'Twenty-five years ago, a team of eight [health care personnel] was in charge of the morning shift; nowadays we have to make do with three' Sonja says. She would like to hear fewer meaningless words from the policymakers and see more decisive action so that government subsidies go entirely to care-giving instead of going to the real estate fund predators.

According to *De Tijd*, the stock market analysts are confident in the economy. The care-related real estate sector is 'corona-proof'. 'Care Property Invest has not been significantly impacted by the pandemic. In early April [2020], it even made its biggest acquisition ever, paying eighty-seven million euros for three Belgian nursing homes. Half of the rental income comes from the OCMW [Public Center for Social Welfare], i.e., from the government.' The real estate investment companies are cashing in. The government is paying. How absurd can it get?

Every Ounce of Prevention is Worth a Pound of Cure

A full two months after contact tracing was started, four out of ten infected people had still not been contacted. Either called too late or not called at all, a completely outdated computer system and call centres failed to detect clusters of infection. And the elementary question 'Whom have you been in contact with and where' was not always asked. This is not a childhood disease, it is a pandemic, but contact tracing appeared to be in a coma in Belgium.

'I can understand the frustrations, but there is nothing I can do about it,' was the answer given by Minister Wouter Beke. He was shifting responsibility to the federal level. 'We were only in charge of finding contact investigators.' Like water sliding off a duck's back, so did his responsibility for the abhorrent situation.

Yet Minister Beke did decide to outsource contact tracing to commercial call centres. Wouter Arrazola de Oñate, director of the Flemish Association for Respiratory Healthcare and a top expert in the field of contact tracing, was appalled: 'In early April [2020] I recommended that it [contact tracing] be carried out by people spread all over Flanders, general practitioners for instance. People who are, at least, a little familiar with the area where the people they are calling live.' Beke ignored Arrazola's recommendation.

'This situation raises some questions we are asking ourselves: what are those Brussels-based contact tracers doing in those call centres? Please take them out into the field, to the front line. And let them help us,' pleads Janneke Ronse to the TV crews. Janneke is the National Chairwoman of Medicine for the People. The doctors for the people were quick to respond and they had been organizing their own system of contact detection and testing ever since April 2020. 'Patients have confidence in us because we are working locally and they know us well', says Janneke. That makes sense, indeed. You are more likely to be willing to entrust your every move to someone you know than to an anonymous caller in a Brussels telephone exchange. 'They're absolutely right. This is the way we have to address this issue,' Arrazola confirms. 'That's the way it should be.'

The members of Medicine for the People are able do so because they operate in group consulting facilities where many people get together, in a collective. In this way, they are able to support one another in the same manner as cycling teams do, taking turns to ward off the severe storm brought about by the virus. In April 2020, they contacted 3,000 patients above the age of seventy, just to ask how they were doing, as a prevention measure. They also asked them whether there was anything they needed?

It is no wonder that the health centres of Medicine for the People are so firmly anchored in the working-class neighbourhoods. They are the first line of the healthcare front, easily accessible to everyone. When the COVID-19 crisis broke out, they switched from doctors' practices to COVID-19 practices at record speed, providing call times and telephone consultations for patients with symptoms. In the front-line zones, they were involved in setting up the first triage stations for hospitals where they carried out the initial screenings in outfits reminiscent of those of cosmonauts.

These were nerve-racking times, but the teamwork was boosting the energy of every healthcare worker. Colleagues provided assistance to fifteen elderly care homes. In Hoboken (Belgium), patients set up a mask-making workshop, by patients for patients. Their diligent work allowed them to make over two thousand masks. In the peak weeks of the crisis, two hundred and fifty volunteers agreed to help Medicine for the People. Homework support was provided in the neighbourhoods for children with learning difficulties. Volunteers became bicycle couriers making home deliveries of medicines and providing shopping and delivery services. The group practices were the social heart of the neighbourhood. It's only normal. But confronted with failing authorities, it becomes a statement by itself.

Prevention is crucial. Prevention actually means making sure people do not get sick. Prevention is better than cure. 'Every ounce of prevention is worth a pound of cure,' Benjamin Franklin said when he was mayor of Philadelphia. An ounce is the equivalent of 28.34 grams and a pound is the equivalent of about 450 grams. In those days, Franklin was talking about fire prevention. Much cheaper, he knew, than having to extinguish a fire.

* * *

We are learning from the experience in Kerala, a state at the southern tip of the great Indian triangle, the truth of Franklin's assertion. In mid-July 2020, India reported one million infections and over twenty-five thousand deaths from COVID-19. Given that context, what has been achieved in Kerala is remarkable. By then, only fifty people out of a population of thirty-five million had died in the state. The secret lies in the strong basic healthcare system.

Each district and each village have their own health centre, managed by the local government. These centres are reinforced by as many as 26,000 prevention workers, almost all of them women. They organize information classes in the neighbourhoods about healthy eating habits and other preventive measures. They offer support to pregnant women; they counsel the elderly; and they make home visits. In short, they work preventively. They know every nook and cranny in the neighbourhood and endeavour to see to it that people don't get sick.

Kerala did take the initial warnings from China seriously and immediately swung into action. Once the COVID-19 pandemic had broken out, it was of the utmost importance not to let the fire spread. 'Break the chain', that is, break the infection chain. The prevention workers monitored all residents in every neighbourhood. Showing symptoms? Not leaving home anymore? They were immediately tested. And people were swiftly put into quarantine as a preventive measure. This was a very efficient system. The prevention workers were also called in to keep the lockdown as bearable as possible. They ensured home delivery of meals, provided shelter for stranded cross-border workers from other regions, and operated mental health helplines. You name it, they did it. This is preventive medicine as part of a comprehensive primary healthcare.

The whole strategy was developed by Kerala's Health Minister, K.K. Shailaja. She is quite an amazing woman and is called the 'Coronavirus Slayer' everywhere today. The *Washington Post* came to the scene and *The Guardian* wrote an article about her work, describing this 63 year-old lady as a kind of rock star. As she herself said, she was particularly happy with the support and cooperation she got from her local population.

* * *

In Belgium, however, it was clear to all that we lagged behind from the very beginning. Holidaymakers back from the spring holiday were not tested. The TV documentary programme Pano revealed that the option chosen was to keep the number of tests as low as possible. Protective gear for the general practitioners who had to carry out the tests was in short supply, so the brakes were applied. The experts were calling for mobile test teams to be set up to visit patients at home and take samples. Such a proposal was rejected because it was 'too costly'. But 'you cannot extinguish a fire with a blindfold on,' the World Health Organization said. It called on all policymakers to test as much as possible.

Whereas tens of thousands of prevention workers were activated in Kerala, in Belgium, staff needed to contain the virus from the start were in short supply, not only for testing, but also for monitoring patients. It is important to monitor members of the household and close contacts in the days following an infection. It is the only way to quickly get rid of the virus. This is standard procedure in measles, tuberculosis, scabies, and other infectious diseases. But at the outbreak of the crisis, only twenty people were working on infection control for Flanders and, amazing as it may seem, there was only one physician-health inspector per province. These people were working themselves to the bone, but they were fighting a losing battle.

More prevention is needed. This is what scientists have been advocating for so long. Back in October 2019, dozens of doctors, deans, and professors had pleaded for more investment in preventive care: 'The healthcare budget stands at several tens of billions of euros. Less than three miserable percent of this goes to prevention, i.e., preventing people from becoming ill. It seems strange that such a tiny part of the budget should go to what is the people's greatest concern. We call on the negotiators of the new federal government to increase the percentage to five percent. This is recommended if we want to come close to countries that are taken as examples.'

In ordinary healthcare, every euro invested in prevention returns four euros of healthcare cost reduction, Professor of Health Economics Lieven Annemans argued. No one responded. On the contrary, the brand-new regional Jambon government announced that prevention institutions such as the Suicide Line, Sensoa (the Flemish Expert Organisation on Sexual Health and HIV), and the Tropical Institute, which has a great deal of expertise on pandemics, will henceforth have to function with fewer resources. The wallet has been closed for prevention in Belgium.

The 1978 Alma Ata Declaration is a milestone in the history of the World Health Organization. It focuses on the model of low-threshold public community health centres that integrate basic care and prevention into their work. This model is now in the process of disappearing. As early as two years later, in 1980, newly elected US President Ronald Reagan opposed this preventive health vision. He called it 'The shortest way to socialism'. Reagan was spurred on by the economic hardliners of the Chicago School, the cradle of neoliberalism. The big money lobbies do not like to see so much healthcare money remaining public. They want to open up the healthcare sector to allow private commercial enterprises free rein. Thinking in terms of health is replaced by thinking in terms of profit, and that leaves no space for prevention. Profit cannot be generated from healthy people.

With the COVID-19 crisis, a cast-iron demonstration of the failure of this neoliberal approach to healthcare has been demonstrated. But nowhere as clearly as in Reagan country where, by mid-July 2020, they had already been forced to store as many as 140,000 coffins, with no prospect of improvement.

Pandemics are Pivotal Moments

In 1854, a cholera epidemic was raging through the working-class districts of London. People were dying like flies and it was unclear why. At that time, the scientific world did not yet use the term bacterium, and numerous vague theories about foul contagious air or miasma were circulating. John Snow was a determined doctor who did not believe any of this. He used to make house calls and kept a meticulous record of his patients' activities. He discovered that almost all cases of this unidentified disease were linked to one single water pump in the Soho district. He arranged for the pump to be shut down. The epidemic did subside. Afterwards, reconnecting the pump was followed by a rebound in the disease.

The findings about contaminated drinking water and the importance of hygiene had no impact upon policy-making until after Dr. Snow's death. They were the basis of the sanitary revolution in Europe. A safe drinking water supply, efficient sewers, and better hygiene, had proven to be essential in ensuring that major cities stayed cholera-free and that life expectancy increased.

International sanitary conferences were held for the first time in the aftermath of the cholera epidemic. These led to an international agreement that from then on countries would be obliged to report outbreaks of infectious diseases such as cholera, the plague, and yellow fever. In addition, it was 'prohibited' for countries to withhold health information for economic or trade reasons.

Nearly three quarters of a century later, in 1918, a new pandemic swept the globe, the Spanish flu. It had nothing to do with Spain as the disease came to Europe during the First World War alongside the US troops. The 'Pale Rider', as it has been named, claimed between fifty and one hundred million lives, i.e., between 2.5 and 5% of the world's population. By comparison, the First World War claimed the lives of eighteen million people.

British author Laura Spinney writes: 'The health authorities then drew an important lesson from the catastrophe: it was unreasonable to point the finger at an individual for being contaminated. Many governments then accepted the concept of universal medicine with free health insurance for all. Russia was at the forefront with a centralised public health system financed by state-owned health insurance. A number of Western European countries followed suit. The US took a different path. And thus, the Spanish flu pandemic, like the cholera pandemic in 1854, became a turning point in the management of medicine.'

The Spanish flu demonstrated that a virus does not roam about with a passport and that it does not care about either language or borders. International cooperation was the only possible response to the pandemic, and an International Agency for the Control of Epidemics was born in Vienna in 1919, as a precursor to the World Health Organization.

COVID-19 too has shown that we all depend on the way diseases are handled in other countries. A local outbreak of an infectious disease can become a global problem in no time. This is why it is in all of our interests to invest in a joint approach. This has always been the mission of international health organizations. The development of these organizations has also always been closely linked to the fight against epidemics.

The World Health Organization (WHO) was established in 1948 as part of the United Nations. At that time, member states were assisting in the financing of the health organisation with a fixed contribution based on their population and wealth, expressed in terms of domestic product. Richer countries contributed more. For specific projects, a second source of income was used, voluntary contributions. The 1980s, however, saw the freezing of fixed contributions. From then on, the health organization often had to beg for monies from countries, agencies, and charities. This is why powerful donors, such as the Bill and Melinda Gates Foundation, have increased decision-making power as to where the money goes. Unfortunately, these monies do not always go to the organization's core tasks.

Remco van de Pas is a researcher in global healthcare at the Tropical Institute in Antwerp. 'The major Western donors set the agenda,' he says. 'The World Health Organization's autonomy to make its own decisions has been curtailed. This also makes the WHO financially dependent and renders it difficult for them to formulate positions.'

More could be done with greater transparency and efficiency. A lot of criticism may be leveled at the World Health Organization. During this precarious time, however, those who would like to weaken it would be banking on mankind committing Harakiri. It is clear that if one country loses the battle against the virus, all countries will lose it. This point of view – collaboration and interdependency – is diametrically opposed to the absurd and deadly logic of 'our-country-first' espoused by nationalists such as Trump and Bolsonaro who have attacked the WHO; a logic that is followed by the right-wing 'populist' party Vlaams Belang (VB) in Belgium.

'In times of contagion, we are one single organism; a community that comprises the whole of mankind' Paolo Giordano, a talented Italian writer who is also a physicist, writes. He is right. The behaviour and the consequences of this virus have taught us that we all belong to one world community. Dr. Ngozi Okonjo-Iweala, the then chairwoman of the international vaccine alliance Gavi, shares this view: 'This crisis has taught me three things. First of all, we are highly interconnected and dependent on each other. We are also incredibly vulnerable. Even the richest countries have been completely caught off guard by this crisis. And finally, this is our last chance to act. We need to invest now in strong healthcare systems and a strong World Health Organization. We should have done that a long time ago. That would have cost a lot less than what we are now losing to this pandemic. And there will be more in the future. As long as there is even so much as one single weak health system, everyone is at risk.'

The Asian Approach

'European leaders should become more modest. For many Europeans, it is still completely inconceivable that anything can be learned from East Asian countries.' Kishore Mahbubani remarks sternly. This Asian intellectual served as Singapore's representative to the United Nations for many years. He has seen a lot and remained silent for a long time. He is disturbed by the arrogance of people who wallow in self complacency. 'In Europe, many people are convinced that their system is superior in all respects.'

Not wanting to learn from Asia's experience has resulted in a significant time loss in the fight against COVID-19. It is not that simple, though, to speak of an 'Asian approach'. The territory concerned is vast, with very different countries, each of them with a very different approach. While in China whole cities quickly went into lockdown, this was hardly the case in Japan and South Korea. The South Koreans were testing on a large scale; the Japanese were testing sparingly. So, what exactly is the 'Asian approach'?

In early March 2020, a few experts published their findings in the renowned medical journal *The Lancet*. The scientists drew three lessons: First, an integrated healthcare system will allow you to better absorb and withstand a shock. Second, trust in science is essential. And third, the trust that patients, healthcare providers, and the population have placed in good government is of paramount importance for a health crisis to be handled properly.

Canadian virologist Bruce Aylward, who travelled to China for two weeks in February 2020 on a World Health Organization mission, was impressed by the rapid reorganization of the healthcare system there. Patients with symptoms of COVID-19 were immediately referred to separate hospitals for testing. Pending the results, they were not allowed to go home. The results were obtained within four hours; in Belgium results still take several days even after months of crisis. Anyone who tested positive was isolated immediately. Patients with mild symptoms were not admitted to the hospital; they were sent to specially equipped care centres. This bold approach was successful.

In Japan, the focus was on identification of clusters, local outbreaks. With each new case, the source of infection was quickly traced in order to break the chain of infection and nip the outbreak in the bud. For this purpose, Japan relied on a network of 450 local health centres, the Hokenjo. Prior to the pandemic, these centres focused on prevention. They can be compared to Belgium's 'Kind en Gezin' (Childhood and Family centres), though they address people of all ages. They are in charge of vaccinating children, investigating complaints of child abuse, giving dietary and sports advice to the elderly, and controlling hygiene in bars and restaurants. They have now been put in charge of contact tracing as well.

In South Korea, mass testing and contact tracing were and continue to be the cornerstone of the strategy to control the virus. Immediately after the outbreak in Wuhan, the Korean prevention centres started a race against time to make test kits. As early as 7 February 2020, the testing programme was rolled out across the country. What a difference from the bungling in Belgium where, months after the outbreak, the system of testing and tracing is still not running smoothly. It is true that the South Koreans had experienced this type of situation in 2015, when another virus, the MERS virus, travelled all over the country and it took two months to get the outbreak under control. Yet we too could have learned from that experience, couldn't we? How come we are still not able to do this?

* * *

On Tuesday, 7 January 2020, Wuhan lab virologist Dr. Shi Zhengli, who has been pursuing viruses in bats for sixteen years, confirmed that some of the lung infections investigated there were caused by a new virus: Sars-CoV-2 (COVID-19). There was a 96% match between its genetic material and that found by Shi Zhengli in horseshoe bats. Four days later, the scientist passed on all the information to the World Health Organization. By then, it had already become clear that there was a close link between the outbreak and a market in Wuhan. Five days after receiving the results of the research, the World Health Organization shared the genetic sequence of the new virus with the whole world. On Thursday 30 January 2020, it declared a 'Global Health Emergency'.

Most Asian countries responded immediately. In Europe, however, there was a prevailing sense of invulnerability. Nevertheless, as early as the end of January 2020, the first infections were detected in France. At the beginning of February, a Belgian citizen repatriated from Wuhan and tested positive. This was the first case of contagion in Belgium.

On Sunday 23 February 2020, the Italian army started the lockdown of eleven cities in Lombardy, and the following day the Italian stock exchange collapsed. Five days later, the Italian government activated the European emergency protocol for aid, the Civic Protection Mechanism. What followed was a painful silence. No help was sent in. Over the weekend of 1 March, holidaymakers returned from ski resorts in Austria's Tyrol and Italy's Tyrol-Sud with 'suitcases full of virus'. That Sunday, the country went into phase two of the emergency plan.

In that very first week of March, there was a growing awareness that a huge health storm was coming. Federal and regional emergency meetings were held. The dramatic scenes from Italian hospitals hit the headlines. In Italy, elderly patients were refused access to overcrowded corridors. In the churches around Bergamo, church pews remained filled with coffins for days. On Sunday 8 March 2020, Italy already had almost ten thousand cases of infection and more than 460 casualties. The country went into lockdown.

The Asian Approach

On that very same day, Bart De Wever attended the premiere of Mamma Mia in the Antwerp Sportpaleis in a canary yellow Abba outfit and bell bottoms. 'All that business has prompted me to send a signal: Yeah, just go out. Just be your normal self! With 50,000 tickets sold, you can't just order such a musical to be cancelled.' This is what De Wever said on VTM, a Belgium commercial television channel. In his opinion, the cancellation of mass events in Italy was an exaggerated move: 'Well now, all the doctors I know, and I know a lot of them, in my party and in my circle of friends, are very annoyed at the wave of panic that has been created regarding COVID-19. But no one dares to say this because its danger should not be minimized either.'

Just be your normal self! Those words typify a certain life outlook. Of course, at that time it was not possible for everyone to be aware of everything. Yet one should expect some caution from those in power. The precautionary principle, you know.

Richard Horton was exasperated by such a pedantic macho attitude. British Prime Minister Boris Johnson was running all over the place trying to sell the same idea. Horton has been Editor-in-Chief of the prestigious scientific magazine *The Lancet* for a quarter of a century. Professor Horton is a kind and nonjudgmental person; but as a doctor, he was disheartened with so much Western denial. He has written a book about it: 'The COVID-19 Catastrophe'.

In his book, he scrutinized each sequence of the crisis. He writes that the stubborn refusal to turn our eyes towards China led to a considerable loss of valuable time. We have witnessed a 'high surge of xenophobia against China,' he explains. People thought that science in China was not on par with the science in the West. This 'arrogance' has been 'responsible for tens of thousands of casualties', because so much time has been wasted. 'On 24 January [2020], when we published the first article on COVID-19 in *The Lancet*, we already knew. We knew that we had to distribute emergency equipment; that we had to apply the principle of testing, tracing, and isolating; we knew that we had to increase the capacity of the intensive care units. And what was done in February to get ready? Nothing, absolutely nothing!'

In 2002-2003, when the SARS virus broke out, China first denied the problem and scientists kept silent, Horton states. 'The contrast with the reaction to this crisis is enormous. The Chinese scientific community mobilized very quickly. By the end of January, we had a complete description of the disease; we knew the genetic sequences; and we knew that the disease is spread from person to person. We also knew that we were going to have a pandemic ripping through the world. All that in barely a month's time.'

Professor Horton believes that all of this should not be brushed aside: 'The humiliation of China by President Trump and others must be carefully investigated. Because, from the point of view of science and public health, the criticism of China and the World Health Organization is totally unfair. I can only explain this by the fact that Western governments, especially those of the United States, are desperately trying to divert attention from their own catastrophic mistakes.'

The facts seem to confirm this. Donald Trump was far behind in all the polls for the American presidential elections. And that is certainly not due to Joe Biden's charisma. Trump's former campaign advisor, Steve Bannon, wonders about the possibility of turning the tide. The right-wing extremist leader had a surprising tip for the The Donald team: 'Keep your mouth shut about Donald Trump,' he said, 'and attack China instead.' Thus, the campaign strategy: Not a word about the candidate himself. Forget Trump. Blame it all on China.

Rather a Body Cream than a Vaccine

American doctor Peter Jay Hotez is a striking figure: solid mustache, always wearing a bow tie, and sporting round-framed glasses. Hotez, a renowned vaccine scientist, is the dean of the National School of Tropical Medicine in Houston, Texas. After the outbreak of the SARS virus, scientists started research to develop a vaccine. Years later, in 2016, Peter Jay Hotez's team finally completed the development of such a vaccine. As this vaccine looked promising, it was decided to produce 20,000 doses of the vaccine to be tested on humans. A research facility at the US Ministry of Defence produced the doses, but what happened with them – nothing. Not a single agency or a single pharmaceutical company was interested in testing the vaccine. 'We looked hard for investors or grants to take the research to the clinical phase. Yet nobody was interested,' Hotez explained. The SARS outbreak in 2016 had already 'gone' so the virus was no longer on the priority list.

'It is easy to deflect the attention of industry. It tends to be a little bit like a kids' soccer game. When the ball goes off in one direction, all the little kids run after it; and then the ball moves in a different direction, and all the little kids run after it again' Mr. Hotez said.

Industry does not run after a ball, of course, it runs after money. In 2016, vaccines against the strain were not expected to be a big money maker. Scientists developed as many as eighty-four candidate vaccines for SARS and MERS all of which were put in a freezer, one after the other.

Vaccines are preventive, and are taken to reduce the chance of infection. When the disease is already present, drugs, 'pharmaceutical products' like antivirals, are taken as treatment.

The development of antivirals is very similar to that of vaccines.

Johan Neyts, internationally renowned virologist at the University of Leuven explains. 'We already knew [about] six viruses, two of them dangerous, SARS and MERS. If we had invested in a virus inhibitor against those known variants, that virus inhibitor might have been effective against COVID-19 as well. In the first weeks after the outbreak in Wuhan it would have been possible to treat those few hundreds of patients, thereby nipping the outbreak in the bud.'

Eleven years ago, I wrote in my book, 'Op Mensenmaat' (On a Human Scale) that out of the latest 1,393 drugs brought to market, only thirteen were intended for tropical diseases such as Malaria; while only four for the treatment of TB, though this disease is affecting the majority of the world's population. Seven of the largest pharmaceutical companies are spending less than one percent of their total research budget on common diseases such as TB and malaria. Big Pharma's business model is at odds with the prevailing needs of the world's population. Tropical diseases in countries with little purchasing power are just not interesting if obscene profit is to be generated, as is the case with the pharmaceutical industry. In poorer countries, people just don't have enough money to purchase pharmaceuticals. Even a vaccine, which would prevent disease and that a patient would only need once or a few times annually, is not interesting in that profit model.

Big Pharma would rather scavenge on wealthy patients it can hold in its grip much longer. Heart medication, addictive tranquilizers, and treatments for male impotence, these are the blockbusters, the money makers. In addition, pharmaceutical giants are increasingly preying on their 'niche busters'. Drugs targeting a specific niche that they can sell at monopoly prices.

Zolgensma is one of those expensive niche busters. Though we may have forgotten the name of that drug, we still remember baby Pia, with the rare degenerative neuromuscular disease Spinal Muscular Atrophy (SMA). This is one of the stories that hit the headlines in 2019 in Belgium. As a result of a million text messages, financial support in the amount of two million euros, and parents who went through fire and hell for Pia, she received her medication.

Despite the fact that the drug was available in the US, it was not yet approved by the EU health department. So, her parents had to raise 1.9 million euros for the injection and the trip to the US so she could be administered the drug. Nearly two million euros for one injection, this is how much it cost. Producer Novartis 'defended their price' by insisting on the high costs involved in research, while keeping quiet about the fact that the scientific breakthrough had not been made by them, but by Genethon, a public research laboratory that, ironically, is financed through crowdfunding from the general public. Novartis bought the patent in 2018 and launched Zolgensma. According to observers it was worth 2.1 billion euros annually!

'It is a misconception that our industry, or any industry, sets the price of a product with the intention of recouping research and development costs,' the former CEO of pharma giant Pfizer said frankly. The pharmaceutical industry invests only a little more than one percent of its revenues into fundamental research for innovative medicines. No, the research budget does not set the price. It is the market that sets the price. The more desperate the patients, the more expensive the drug. This is cold logic.

On the radio, I heard Hans Maertens of Voka (Chamber of Commerce and Industry in Flanders) warn that the economic costs of COVID-19 are huge. He was already estimating them at forty to sixty billion euros. Every additional week meant extra economic damage. And that prediction was made in mid-April 2020. What will this economic devastation look like in Europe? What will it look like in the rest of the world? A fraction of the hundreds of billions of euros lost would have been sufficient for research into a vaccine. Today, no one should blunder about the large amounts of money needed for research, testing, and production. It is an expensive process, of course, but it's a pittance as compared to the dramatic costs of the pandemic now and into the future.

It is preposterous that the development of a new body cream should take precedence over that of a vaccine. It is deadly that Big Pharma should have sweeping control over our health; but it is a political choice. It is inexcusable that public money is made available for research and development and then the results are patented by private companies; but it is a political choice. Who can still be defending these choices today given the impact of this global pandemic?

Could You Patent the Sun?

Poliomyelitis, i.e., infantile paralysis, is a serious infectious disease. It can be spread by coughing and sneezing, direct contact, or through contaminated food or water. Ever since the polio vaccination became compulsory in the 1960's, polio has almost disappeared.

There is no treatment for polio, but there is a preventive: a vaccine. This vaccine is named after the American virologist Jonas Edward Salk. Polio was a major health scourge; Dr. Salk fought it. Together with his team he dedicated himself to this task for years and was finally able to try the vaccine successfully on animals in 1952. Two years later the vaccine was tested on over a million schoolchildren, the 'polio pioneers'. Twenty-thousand doctors and public health personnel were involved in the operation. The vaccine was safe. Dr. Salk became a national hero.

The scientist shunned all attention. 'Young man, a great tragedy has befallen you: you have lost your anonymity', the famous TV anchor, Ed R. Murrow, told him. Then Murrow asked him: 'Who owns the patent on this vaccine?' Dr. Salk calmly replied, 'Well, the people, I would say. There is no patent. Could you patent the sun?'

Salk did not let himself be carried away by self-interest or profit-seeking. He did not believe that health science should be tethered to patents. The polio vaccine was made available without a patent. It is affordable, and nowadays the disease has been eradicated in large parts of the world.

A universal response to a universal threat, and it should be no different today. On 10 January 2020, Chinese scientists put the genetic code of the virus online. Ten seconds later, quite literally, thousands of scientists took up the job worldwide. They worked around the clock, at a feverish pace, to try and develop a vaccine and test drugs for the treatment of COVID-19. Such a collective approach, on a global scale, is rarely observed.

In this pandemic, we have to make sure that the results of all this research in labs all over the world, also remains in the public domain; that when this gigantic collective effort is over, the results will not be monopolised by the pharmaceutical giants.

Fear of the pharmaceutical giants stealing the research is more than justified. One of those giants is Gilead. In March 2020, this American company hurriedly applied for 'orphan-drug' status for Remdesivir. This category includes drugs against rare diseases. Such a certification is extremely lucrative: it gives the proprietor an exclusive marketing right for a period of seven years, additional subsidies, and tax breaks. Just before Remdesivir's certification by Gilead, the World Health Organization declared Remdesivir to be one of the most promising drug candidates for the treatment of COVID-19.

At this stage, one can say a lot about COVID-19, but certainly not that it is a rare virus. Gilead, nonetheless, managed to secure Remdesivir in the nick of time, given that the pandemic had not yet broken out in the United States in March. But things did not happen as they had expected. Public outcry was such that Gilead had to double back. The company withdrew its application.

Yet the saga is far from over. As long as profit beckons, morals are non-existent. At the end of June 2020, Gilead announced that one vial of the drug would cost $390. As a result, a standard six-vial pack would cost $2,340; whereas real production costs amounted to a mere $6. The market price was four hundred times more than the production costs for the drug.

One should also be aware of the fact that the drug was originally developed with public funding, amounting to hundreds of millions of dollars, as a potential treatment for Hepatitis C, and later on Ebola. Gilead purchased it after it had been developed and developed it further with large amounts of public funds from the National Institute of Health.

Could You Patent the Sun?

'With COVID-19, it is now painfully obvious that monopolization comes at the cost of human lives.' This is what Nobel Prize winner in economics Joseph Stiglitz wrote, referring to Remdesivir and the behaviour of monopolies when it came to testing. He explained how the 441 patents held by 3M had hampered large-scale production of face masks. 'If we let pharmaceutical companies have their way, not everyone will have access to the vaccines', he concluded.

* * *

The pharmaceutical industry has been lobbying for three decades in order to see its intellectual property rights strictly enforced at a national level and to anchor such rights at an international level. Pharmaceutical giant Pfizer and the then CEO Edmund Pratt, in particular, managed to persuade the US government to make patents a key issue at the World Trade Organization. In 1994, they got what they wanted with the agreement on Trade-Related Aspects of Intellectual Property Rights (TRIPS). This agreement was largely tailored to their needs. The impact on countries in the southern hemisphere has been severe. The prescribed therapy for HIV costs $10,000 per year, per patient, and the new agreements closed the door to cheaper generic alternatives.

A few years before the TRIPS agreement was signed, the situation in South Africa was exploding. The country had only recently shaken off the yoke of the longstanding apartheid and had to then come to grips with the outbreak of AIDS. Every day as many as 1,000 South Africans died from the consequences of the HIV infection. Five million South Africans were infected, i.e., almost one eighth of the total population.

The South African government had been dilly dallying for a long time, but now Nelson Mandela and the National African Congress could no longer ignore the outbreak. South Africa endorsed the Medicines and related Substances Control

Amendment Act. This piece of legislation laid down the obligation for patent-holders to grant compulsory licences to companies on the generic market to produce cheaper drugs. These compulsory licences made the import of generic HIV medicines possible. A way to tackle the medical emergency with which the country was faced had been found at last.

This wasn't to Big Pharma's liking, though. In 1998, thirty-nine pharmaceutical multinationals started legal proceedings against the Mandela government. The multinationals were supported by the US's Clinton administration and the European Commission. The public reacted furiously and strongly supported Mandela. The legal document entitled 'Thirty-nine drug companies versus Nelson Mandela' provided sufficient evidence for this support. The ongoing protest forced the US government to back off. Finally, the pharmaceutical giants also dropped the case. Big Pharma was left empty-handed for the first time in South Africa.

Today, not only South Africa, but the whole planet is in a similar situation. Is an accessible and affordable vaccine against COVID-19 for everyone going to be available or not? Canada, Chile, and Ecuador have announced that they too are ready to impose compulsory licences if necessary. It is possible in Belgium, but the government is hesitant.

The resources to fight a universal evil should be universal – without patents and monopolies on life-saving vaccines, antibiotics, and antivirals. This should become the standard not only in today's pandemic, but also for future pandemics. 'It always seems impossible until it's done,' Mandela said. It always seems impossible until we do it.

They Have Forgotten Us

PART III

The Looming Crisis

'There is no need to bow,' said Prometheus,
touching one of them
and marveling at the robustness
and life he could feel pounding within.
'Excuse me,' said Zeus: 'there is every need to bow. We are their gods.'
'I am not their god,' said Prometheus, . . . 'I am their friend.'
The more he watched over
and mingled with his creation, the more Prometheus became convinced
that fire was exactly what they needed.
Fire, real hot, fierce, flickering, flaming fire,
to enable them to melt, smoulder, bake, roast,
stew, mould, and forge.
And they needed an inner creative fire too, a divine fire,
to enable them to think, imagine, and dare.

Stephen Fry, 'Mythos'

On the other side of the planet someone ate a strange animal and three months later half of mankind was quarantined. The virus travelled around the world in 100 days. It was silent and merciless. A silent killer arrived, but without anyone noticing that it was already present. Billions of people were compelled to live behind closed doors and distrust each other. The virus was in town.

The tiny COVID-19 struck like a meteorite, the impact of which smashes things to smithereens, as was already known sixty million years ago. In those days, the impact of one such meteorite was so severe that dinosaurs did not survive it. They were hardy animals, though.

The hardy animals of our time are the giant ocean shipping companies. They sail around the planet filled with containers. If you want to know how the economy is doing, just look at the ships, my father said. If they are fully laden and low in the water, all is well; if they are high in the water, there are problems. Today's ships are high in the water; many containers are filled with air.

In 2020, some 170 out of 195 countries experienced negative growth. This means that the situation in over ninety percent of countries has and continues to deteriorate. Even after the Wall Street crash of 1929, such economic devastation did not happen. It has been calculated that by the end of 2020, twelve percent of all working hours will be lost, which amounts to a loss of 340 million full-time jobs. All this devastation, due to the inability and unwillingness to deal globally and systemically with this virus particle that measures a mere 125 nanometers!

The peculiarity of this crisis is that it affects both the supply side and the demand side of economic activity. That governments had to shut down production chains, transport networks, distribution systems, and commercial markets was unprecedented. The International Monetary Fund is referring to 'The Great Lockdown' as comparable to the Great Depression a century ago. The system had to put itself into a coma for a while in order to be able to survive.

An impact creates a crater. After the impact, however, the crater can be filled. It is said that this will be the case now as well. The picture we have seen is that of a V-shaped drop and recovery. This translates into a deep fall of about 10 percent of production in the western world for 2020 and continuing for some time into 2021. This could be followed by an almost equal rebound, the likes of which can only be seen in bungee jumping. In the event of another wave, one could expect a W-shaped drop and recovery: twice into the ravine, twice back up.

The prognosis is that most of the world economy – excluding China – is now going to be on a ventilator in intensive care for a while, after which it will be in rehab, and then it may leap forward.

Governments, however, have conveniently forgotten that capitalism was already ill before COVID-19 struck. By mid-2019, the world was already heading for a meltdown. Germany—Germany!—was the first country to dive below zero growth. 'The Inevitability of Recession,' was the headline of *De Tijd* last summer. No one was talking about a new bat virus in the summer of 2019.

There were other indicators of a stagnant economy as well. Demand was sputtering in the automobile, construction, and steel industries. In aviation, oversupply was on the increase. The trade war between the United States and China started getting out of hand.

The world economy never fully recovered from the financial crisis of 2008. It has been bungling on the brink of recession for the past twelve years. Growth was stagnating; investments were lagging; and debts were accumulating. Both the V and W scenarios only measure the impact of the 'bruise' in an otherwise resilient organism. But in fact, the organism was already showing severely impaired resistance.

* * *

We all remember the notorious 2008 banking crisis. How an exuberant party of investment bankers, hedge fund managers, and venture capitalists manipulating the financial markets, resulted in the collapse of the global economy like a house of cards.

Authorities had to step in. The major banks were declared too big to be allowed to fail and their losses were nationalised. Since then, we have come to know that nationalisations are taboo, except when the debts of investors and speculators are concerned. We have also come to know that juggling with repackaged mortgage loans and other toxic financial products is not illegal. No hedge fund capitalist was put behind bars: too big to jail.

Public debt, used to cover the losses of reckless investment bankers, went through the roof everywhere. The address on the bill was not the Cayman Islands; the bill was sent directly to Joe Public. For twelve years now, blind austerity measures, under the banner of 'reduce the deficit' decreased funding for healthcare, nursing homes, scientific research, strategic stocks of protective equipment, and so on.

'Pruning for growth', neoliberal parrots kept squawking in a myriad of ways. The engine of recovery, however, continued to sputter, growth rates were driven to zero, and debts remained at very high levels. The neoliberal miracle model doesn't work at all. What's the answer to this? Fresh money! Central banks and governments worldwide injected the exorbitant amount of four trillion euros into the economy. Central bankers were telling us with a lot of flair that they would boost the snail's pace growth through monetary policy. If we kept turning on the tap over and over again, if we kept lowering interest rates further and further, and fertilised the earth's surface with free money, new productive investments would be ubiquitous. This is what was and is still being said.

The problem is that the funds have not been channeled into the intended investments. They are flowing to other places. A portion of the money remained stuck in large banks that used it to polish up their balance sheets. Another portion was lent out to big business. Yet big business hardly ever uses its mountain of cash for productive investments. It demands double digit profit margins. For anything less, it will not lift a finger. It would rather use that money either to pay high dividends to big shareholders or to buy back its own shares. This is financial cannibalism: The more peers one swallows, the higher the share price rises.

In addition, these scarce investments are often unproductive. For instance, a lot of money is spent on buying up companies or pushing through mega mergers. This is how large monopolies manage to grow still larger.

Moreover, according to the International Monetary Fund's calculations, forty percent of foreign investment by multinationals is in fact a ghost investment. All of these shell companies are created to avoid taxation. The total involved is a dizzying-high amount of fifteen trillion dollars.

This is how these billions end up going back to the speculators. These people continue blowing more artificial bubbles. The more money gets pumped into the banks, the bigger the bubbles and the higher the stock market prices. Yet the growth rate of the real economy is not showing any upward trend, that goes without saying. The New York Stock Exchange had been climbing steadily for twelve years until COVID-19 put an abrupt end to this ascension in mid-March 2020.

In that fateful one week of March 2020, $1.5 trillion worth of fictional wealth went up in smoke. This is a thirteen-digit number; thirteen digits, which make us realize that the stock market crash of 2020 was as important as that of 2008. This time, governments and central banks did not hesitate for a moment to develop a new bonanza of incentives and distribution programmes. The result goes without saying. Speculators immediately came back to the stock market; they were back in business to organize another party. Stock market newspapers were talking about 'the most manic semester ever.' Whereas the world was falling victim to the deadly virus, it hardly took the stock exchange one semester to fall off the edge of the cliff down to the bottom and climb right back up to the top. In stock market jargon: From 'bull market' to 'bear market' and just as quickly back to 'bull market'. The US stock markets exited 2020 with the S&P 500 growing 18% (including dividends), Nasdaq surging 43.6%, and the Dow Jones rising 7.2%. So even as the real economy was locked-down and millions of workers lost their jobs, the top .01% saw their wealth increase exponentially.

When the Mayor of New York Quotes Karl Marx

The New York counterpart of the Belgian public radio channel *De Ochtend op Radio 1* (Morning on Radio 1) is *The Brian Lehrer Show*. On 24 July 2020, New York Mayor Bill de Blasio was a guest on the show.

'That my focus isn't on business and the elite, there's truth in that,' de Blasio said. 'I am tempted to borrow a quote from Karl Marx here.' 'They'll like that on Wall Street,' was the reply given by the interviewer.

'Yes, they will,' de Blasio answered, laughing, 'But there's a famous quote from Karl Marx here.... there is a famous quote that "the state is the executive committee of the bourgeoisie". I actually read that when I was a young person and I said, no, that's not the way it's supposed to be.'

When the economy collapses, strange things do happen. Marx is quoted on the radio. This is no coincidence. For indeed, the greatest enemies of all that is collective today suddenly turn into great lovers of the authorities. Their sudden love for a central authority will help them to recoup their losses. The law will follow, of course. The state must guarantee protection of the common interest of the capitalists. That is what the quote from Marx is about. That's how it was at that time, that's how it was in 2008, and that's how it is again today.

To think that neoliberals do not want government intervention is a popular misconception. Of course, they do, to serve the interests of big money, that is. The state was never far away from the economic sector. The core of neoliberalism is not the relationship between the market and the state, it is total submission of the state to the slavery of capital.

In 2020, central banks and governments pumped 4 trillion

euros into the global economy in order to absorb the crash. 'There was no other choice,' was the collective cry. 'Governments have no choice but to intervene when the market collapses.' In times of crisis and pandemics, everyone is a 'socialist'; but not everyone has access to this brand of socialism.

Just because there is no other way, the European Union was forced to put its harsh and strict budget and debt standards on hold for a while. It opened its purse strings widely. Monopolies, airline companies, automobile manufacturers, and other giants have been granted deferral of payments, guarantees, and umpteen subsidies. Small business, hotels and restaurants, event agencies, artists, the self-employed, fair-ground entertainers, freelancers, caterers, and students were the biggest losers.

Government support costs a lot of money; costs are adding up all over the world. They quickly 'overlooked' a few trillion euros, not to mention bank guarantees and the deferral of payments.

Meanwhile income is considerably reduced. And, as every household knows, he who spends more than he collects will end up in the red. This makes sense. The public authorities call this the government deficit in the annual budget. On a global scale, government deficits in 2020 reached nearly ten percent of global wealth. This means that they will have tripled as compared to 2019. Such is the assessment made by the International Monetary Fund. If you have been in deficit for years on end, debts will have piled up. COVID-related deficits are going to lead to a sharp increase in the world's public debt that will reach levels unheard of in the past 150 years.

* * *

Public authorities, businesses, and households, are in debt. Volkswagen's debt burden, for instance, is almost as large as that of a medium-sized country like South Africa. The total debt of governments, business, and the population amounts to no less than 253 trillion dollars. This is an increase of one hundred trillion dollars in comparison with the 2008 financial crisis. The world's indebtedness now amounts to 322 percent of global production. In other words, in 2020, we already used up as much as we will have to produce for the next three years. Capitalism as a whole, lives on credit.

Such a situation is untenable. The key question will be who's going to pay for all this. The supply side of the economy is expected to recover, production will restart. However, recovery on the demand side raises many more doubts. All three engines that are supposed to drive demand are sputtering: Households invest less and consume less; public authorities are heavily indebted; and the big private companies are clinging to their money in expectation that new markets will open.

In most of Europe, low-income earners and vulnerable households have already been hit, but for most households the shock has yet to come. The government absorbed the first quake through a system of temporary unemployment and transitional support. Once these measures are withdrawn, the doors will slam shut. In Belgium, 100,000 people are expected to have lost their jobs in 2020. Across Europe, there may be more than two million. Half of the world's workers are seeing their livelihoods threatened due to loss of hours worked, loss of wages, or loss of jobs. Consumers have applied the handbrakes. They are being careful. Those who can will save more and spend less. The consumer engine is sputtering.

Authorities did inject money. This, however, is temporary, and is only meant to absorb the first shock and restore supply. Much-needed expenditures, though of a different nature from the major strategic public investments, are indispensable to carry out the ecological transition, to establish an effective preventive healthcare system, and to build a solid infrastructure. Funds also need to be spent on education, culture, scientific research, public order, safety, etc. It is by no means certain that the authorities are going to be willing to make these strategic investments tomorrow now that their indebtedness has gone through the roof and the liberal think-tanks are claiming that this is not the task of government.

The third engine, the one that should have boosted demand, also failed. Many private companies have either cut down on their investment plans, or even called them off. In the field of export, the situation is still too uncertain, the dust has not yet settled. Just as in any other major crisis, there will be winners and there will be losers. The winners are tech companies, computer-science companies, and digital mammoths. Worst affected are airline companies, the catering sector, the tourism industry, construction, and the cultural and event sectors. The crisis has had a brutal cleansing effect. The weakest are going under; the concentration of capital is on the increase; and the high and mighty are grabbing the lion's share of the market without having to invest.

If the plane's three engines start sputtering simultaneously, you'd better bail out, this is just common sense. In this case, however, having a good parachute is vital.

A Tinderbox That Can Set the Prairie on Fire

In many countries of the South, the crisis is more an income crisis than a health crisis. As many as two billion people in the world are employed in the informal sector. So, you will buy food at night with what you are hoping to earn the next day. If you are not allowed on the street with your stall or your pedicab because of the lockdown, you will immediately descend into poverty. It is an impossible situation. If you don't work, you won't have anything to eat. But if you do work, you are at risk of getting infected. According to the Oxfam report, *The Hunger Virus*, the number of people living in hunger will increase with up to 500 million in 2020. Schools have been closed in 192 countries, affecting 1.5 billion young people. Now that many have seen their family's income wiped out, child labour is on the rise again.

By the end of 2020, nearly twenty-five thousand people per day were dying of hunger, according to the UN. More than two million people died from COVID-19 by year's end.

The climate crisis makes the situation even worse. Unpredictable weather conditions are causing poor harvests. Yet, there is more than enough food to feed the entire world population. The top ten food processing multinationals have paid eighteen billion dollars to their shareholders in the first year of the pandemic. That is ten times the amount needed to eliminate global hunger.

'Sunset last night, isolated in the Grenadines avoiding the virus. I'm hoping everybody is staying safe.' This is a tweet that media magnate David Geffen posted in early April 2020. Along with an idyllic photo of his super-yacht that is one hundred and thirty-eight meters long. Quarantine is not the same for everybody. No one can deny anymore that on this planet inequalities take the most obscene forms.

A Tinderbox that Can Set the Prairie on Fire

'While the disease situation in the city is volatile and every minute somebody dies here, wealthy people ask me whether they can have their own intensive care unit installed in their villa and whether I could give them a tip,' says a doctor in New York. Between the boundaries of the extremes, between the wealthiest of the wealthy and the poorest of the poor, the abyss is immeasurably deep. If the richest man on earth were to form a stack with all his one-hundred-dollar bills and sit on top of it like a rooster, he would be sitting outside our stratosphere into outer space. That statement was uttered at the World Economic Forum, certainly not a left-wing club.

It is estimated that another 500 million people will be pushed into deep poverty before this pandemic is over. At the same time, it has been documented that American billionaires have seen their fortunes rise by $500 billion during the crisis. The rich get richer, the poor get poorer, and the gap keeps widening. 'There must be something rotten to the very core of a social system that increases its wealth without diminishing its misery,' Karl Marx said bluntly.

In such a situation, one single spark could set the whole steppe ablaze. Tinderbox is a beautiful English word. It is a box used to light a fire, the forerunner of the matchbox. 'The economic impact of the virus is that of a tinderbox.' This observation is made by analysts at Verisk Maplecroft, a firm that specializes in the analysis of the possibility of civil unrest in different countries.

The consequences of COVID-19 will fuel unrest and instability in many places. The analysts see Nigeria, Iran, Bangladesh, Algeria, and Ethiopia as being at greatest risk of this 'perfect storm'. The virus increases all contradictions. Newspapers foresee 'unparalleled street protests' in at least thirty-seven countries. Big countries such as India, Brazil, and South Africa, too, are buzzing and throbbing, and stability is not guaranteed.

'Nothing is More Permanent than the Temporary'

On Saturday afternoon, 14 March 2020, I got a call from our city alderman Geert Asman in Zelzate. He asked whether we agreed with the closing of the border with the Netherlands? In Belgium, shops, cafes, and restaurants had already closed the night before. Pub regulars found ways to sneak to Terneuzen, Sluis, and Hulst in the Netherlands. The Zeeland authorities were expressing a lot of anger about the arrival of Belgian 'refugees' in the midst of a galloping pandemic, which was leading to unprecedented activity in shopping streets and cafés, in car parks and terraces.

Why was one country closing its shops whereas another was not? Why was the Dutch Ministry of Foreign Affairs advising against travelling to Northern Italy whereas Belgium was not? Why was everything staying open in Malmö, Sweden whereas in Copenhagen, Denmark, hardly one bridge away, everything was locked-down?

The European actors were clearly not aligned at the deadly overture of the great drama. Things had been different, though, on the penultimate day of January 2020 – standing applause, hugs even, and song. We'll meet again, don't know where, and don't know when. These were scenes from the farewell reception for the British in the European Parliament. Those images travelled around the world.

On the same day, Italy banned all flights to and from China. Italy called for a meeting of European health ministers as early as 27 January. It wanted agreements to be established on screening people arriving in Europe. However, Europe brushed away the Italian proposal. More than two weeks went by before the European Health Ministers met on 13 February.

'Nothing is More Permanent than the Temporary'

In those days, Europe was wallowing in self-righteousness, as has been revealed since by the Bureau of Investigative Journalism. The European Commission was still convinced, at that time, that Europe was 'well prepared' for the pandemic. Self-righteousness was inappropriate; the existing contingency plans were outdated; stock levels had dropped; stocks had been destroyed; communication was poor; and everyone was doing as they pleased. It was a bit like Belgium, but on a larger scale, so to speak.

People at the top of the EU thought that COVID-19 was mainly 'a Chinese problem' that would just blow over. It did not blow over. By the end of February 2020, hospitals in Lombardy could not cope with the influx of patients anymore. Italians needed help, they needed it urgently. They needed masks, lots of them. On 26 February, they approached the European Commission for help and protective equipment. The appeal went unheeded. Europe had no stock. In France, stocks of masks had dropped from 1.7 billion units in 2011 to 117 million units when the epidemic broke out. It amounted to ten times less than the original amount, a result of the austerity programmes. In Belgium, the stock had been destroyed and had not been replaced; the major reason for this being budget reductions. In recent years, the European Commission had called on member states exactly sixty-three times to save on healthcare spending. The result of this policy – Italy was moving its dead to mass graves and Europe was stumbling.

* * *

The small virus hit Europe hard. At the end of July 2020, nearly one million Europeans were infected, 200,000 people had died and 1.5 million had recovered. By way of comparison, Asia also had nearly one million infected people at that time, but 'only' 80,000 died and more than 2.5 million had recovered. Europe's economy was also being hit hard by the healthcare crisis. The crisis brought back memories of 1929, but with a bang. Germany was faced with the threat of a six percent slump in production, Spain with a slump of almost eleven percent, and Italy twelve percent. While the worst blow came in the autumn.

The biggest worry was Italy. It was badly hit by COVID-19 and the lockdown. In addition, it saw a steep downturn in revenues from the tourism sector.

Italy is no small beer, though. It is the third largest economy in Europe and the eighth largest in the world, after Germany and France. Despite the clichés and derogatory comments, Rome has long been a net contributor to the European Union. It transfers up to five billion euros annually to Brussels. The industrial basins in northern Italy are strongly interwoven with the German ones; the supply chains run across the Alps. The continuing economic standstill is resulting in a partial fall out for both the German automobile industry and mechanical engineering.

It was high time to act. In mid-July 2020, Italian Prime Minister Giuseppe Conte and German Chancellor Angela Merkel met in the Meseberg baroque castle. They wanted to set up a European Recovery Fund in order to recover from the crisis. Both put forth the same arguments: the risk of the European market collapsing was a threat to everyone. 'Everyone', Giuseppe Conte underlined the word in red. If Italy goes bust, the euro is bound to follow.

And Italy's fall might mean as much for Germany as well. Merkel understood that. Germany was already confronted with a dramatic slowdown in growth even before the pandemic broke out and was the first European country to fall into recession. If southern Europe fell, a large part of the German export market would fall too.

To save the euro, Angela Merkel joined forces with French President Emmanuel Macron. They had already found common ground before the pandemic arrived. Brexit and the impending recession had driven them into each other's arms, just as the common will to put European big industry on the world stage vis-à-vis China and the United States had already done. The bat virus accelerated that process.

It should not be forgotten that, from its inception, the European project has provided a link between German, French, and Italian major companies in their bid to operate in the world market as a European industry. Very recently, at the end of 2019, the German patrons of BDI, the Italian patrons of Confindustria, and the French patrons of Medef (Mouvement des Entreprises de France) came together to present a united front and to demand European investments that would strengthen their position. They want to become international monopolies. They call themselves 'European champions'. It is this industrial axis that determines Europe's policy.

While Belgians were preparing for a low-key national holiday, in the early hours of 21 July 2020, twenty-seven European member states concluded an agreement for a European Recovery Plan. This plan cost the Franco-German tandem blood, sweat, tears, lots of objections, dressing-downs, and four long days and nights. 'Historic event!' could be heard from both sides of the Rhine.

The Recovery Fund put 750 billion euros onto the table to help severely affected countries such as Italy and Spain. Such a thing would have been completely unthinkable ten years ago; but at that very moment it was either this umbrella fund or drowning together. For the first time, member states jointly borrowed money on the international capital markets. Solidarity consists in sharing the risk. If the Italians or Spaniards had to borrow money individually, it would have cost them a lot more than it would have the Germans or the Dutch. A large part of the Recovery Fund was allocated to the worst affected countries. That's logical, one would say, but until then such transfers had been avoided in Europe. As a part of this plan, the European Union would also be able to collect its own taxes.

Joint loans, budgetary transfers, joint income: it was certainly not the same as the 2010 grindstone mechanism. At that time, Athens was all alone when it had to ask for money, and loans were granted with bone-crushing conditions and with worse repayment schedules. This led Greece to quite literally sell lands and treasures to repay the EU. Consequently, the Greek debt issue worsened instead of improving. Imposing such a strategy on Italy today would not only have made the country sink, but it could also have caused a conflagration in the banking sector and threatened the very existence of the euro. The agreement takes a step towards a new brand of federalism. Indeed, the solidarity mechanism is supposed to be 'temporary', but 'nothing is as permanent as the temporary'; people in the European corridors know that.

* * *

'This is a major step in the history of European integration and a clear signal: Even in a crisis situation, we stick together. Together, we take on the competition from China and the US. The European Union acts in unison, we link our destinies.' Those words were uttered by Armin Laschet, Prime Minister of North Rhine-Westphalia who wandered into this book earlier through the meat scandal at Tönnies. Laschet is a candidate to succeed Merkel in the Christian Democratic Union (CDU).

The European Union may well have taken a step forward toward federalism, but at the same time contradictions have been exacerbated. The persistent torpedo salvos launched by the 'frugal four' – the Netherlands, Austria, Denmark, and Sweden – almost blew up the Recovery Fund. They were opposed to any real European solidarity mechanism, with or without the pandemic.

'We're not here to spend the rest of our lives attending each other's birthdays', said the Dutch Prime Minister Mark Rutte during a European summit. Rutte sticks to the old Troika-model (the European Union, the European Central Bank, and the International Monetary Fund). He was demanding that each Member State have a veto right on each transfer. He was resisting transfers. He was demanding the application of hard neoliberal conditions for every loan. Those conditions brought Athens to its knees in 2010. It was never intended that Greece should be rescued; rather it was about rescuing a number of German and French major banks at the expense of the Greek population who are now drowning in permanent debt. I wrote about this in my book 'How Dare They'.

Barely three years ago, Mark Rutte was praised all over Europe for his 'historic' victory over Geert Wilders' right-wing 'populism'. Today, with Wilders' hot breath on his neck, Rutte is demonstrating his core neoliberal chauvinism. The images of Geert Wilders' one-man demonstration through the Binnenhof in The Hague with a sign 'Not a Penny to Italy', were seen in all the news bulletins. Emboldened by this most basic chauvinism, the firebugs at *De Telegraaf* also resumed their hateful campaign against 'the spendthrift garlic countries' of Southern Europe.

It must be said that The Hague can fire this salvo only because Berlin is turning a blind eye. It somehow suited Merkel that Rutte and Denmark, Sweden and Austria would form a sort of Hanseatic League of radicalised northerners ready to lash out during the negotiations. It could be viewed as a 'carrot and stick' diplomacy: Germany 'appeals' for unity while the Netherlands demands harsh monetary terms. Merkel comes out smelling like a rose.

It is a fact that Rutte's wishes were partially met. Although there is no veto clause, the emergency brakes can be applied. Only one country needs to sound the alarm if it feels that another country was not using the money properly. But what does 'good use' mean in times of a pandemic? Opinions differ on that matter. The grant money is also subject to strict conditions. Each member state has to submit a plan and the European Commission signals its approval or rejection of that plan. Let no one have any illusions, the recipes concocted by the neoliberal European governments, with competition as their alpha and omega, remain the norm in all European structures.

The frugal four got even more. They got a lot of praise. Praise in the form of additional cuts in their contributions to the European Union. The fact that those who benefit most from the euro forced such cuts in the midst of Europe's fiercest calamity made many purse their lips.

The Netherlands was granted a deduction of as much as two billion euros. As if nobody knew that behind the mask of 'champion of strict European budgetary rules' there hides a fiscal robber. Research shows that The Netherlands is the most important tax haven for multinationals, right in the centre of Europe. If Fiat's financial headquarters were moved to the Netherlands, Fiat would have hardly paid any taxes, and Italy would lose a large amount in tax revenues. In this way, The Hague will earn three billion euros, while letting its European neighbours lose more than twenty billion euros. Step by step, the European Union appears to be moving forward, but with each step the cracks in the house are getting bigger.

Is All That Money Going to Those Who Need It?

All sorts of fire-fighting operations were needed to absorb the worst shocks and to attempt to get the economy back on track. The 750 billion euros from the European Recovery Plan were complemented by the European Central Bank's money spigot. The latter has injected no less than 1.35 trillion euros into the economy by purchasing government bonds. The fact that the central bank also purchased corporate bonds is less known. Among others, it purchased debt securities from Shell, Total, and the luxury-products group Moët Hennessy Louis Vuitton (LVMH). It did not seem to be bothered by the fact that these multinationals are known planet polluters and reputed tax-evaders.

In addition, national administrations were drawing up their own rescue plans. It is only logical for an administration to intervene in order to prevent business failures and to attempt the rescue of as many jobs as possible. There is a significant difference, however, between the current crisis and the crash of 2008. At that time, the crash had been caused by speculation on financial markets, i.e., people were implicated; this time, the crisis has been caused by a virus from outside the human community.

Yet a frightening amount of parallels can be drawn between the rescue packages of the past and those of today. Just as before, by far the largest amount of money went to big business. Restaurant owners, freelancers, singers, and the self-employed had to compete for what was left. This type of relief is something one sees almost everywhere these days. It raises two questions: Was the money really going exclusively to big companies that would not survive without government support? And what conditions had to be met in order to get the money?

During lockdown, the Belgian government stepped in and granted more than a million people, i.e., forty percent of the workforce in the private sector, a partial unemployment allowance. The German government stepped in for seven million employees; the French government adjusted lost wages for as many as eleven million employees. This was desperately needed support.

The first question is: was all that taxpayers' money directed only to companies that would go out of business without such support? The answer is no.

Automobile manufacturer BMW was sitting on a cash reserve of more than twelve billion euros and in 2019 it paid out dividends in the amount of 1.6 billion euros to its shareholders. Half of that amount went to two individuals, brother and sister Stefan Quandt and Susanne Klatten. They are among the richest people on the planet. In March 2020, BMW put twenty thousand workers on partial temporary unemployment, 'Kurzarbeit' in German. The German government paid for that. Isn't that obscene? How can a company with a money reserve of billions of euros and a dividend bonanza for shareholders at the same time apply for state aid?

In 2020, not only BMW, but also Volkswagen paid dividends to their shareholders. Volkswagen even went so far as to shamelessly increase its dividends by three billion euros. At Siemens, dividends were increased by sixty percent in 2020, as if there was no crisis at all. In addition, the company is continuing to buy back its shares. Meanwhile, three thousand Siemens workers are on Kurzarbeit, supported by the government.

If you have enough cash to lavish shareholders with billions, surely you must be able to continue to pay employees' wages during a pandemic emergency? It appears, however, that the intentions of the corporate managers at BMW, Volkswagen, and Siemens are to secure dividends rather than jobs. All the government's money was basically stolen and reached neither small business nor pub owners, hairdressers, artists, shopkeepers or bakers; those who really do need it in order not to disappear once and for all.

Is All That Money Going to Those Who Need It?

The second question is what conditions are attached to state aid? The answer, there are none.

We had a good fight about that in the Belgian parliament as well. A measure was approved aimed at refusing tax deferrals to big businesses that relied on tax avoidance procedures That was great! Just before the bell rang however, and through the back door, liberals and social democrats inserted a protective loophole in the provision. It provided that companies, which perform transactions with tax havens, will not receive support unless they do so 'for legitimate financial or economic needs'. Can you believe this? Of course, they avoid taxes for legitimate financial needs! After all, tax avoidance is perfectly legitimate, it is legal. We introduced an amendment calling for the closure of the loophole, but it was voted down.

A missed opportunity, because in 2019, 800 Belgian companies transferred 172 billion euros to accounts in tax havens such as Bermuda and the Cayman Islands, for tax evasion purposes. How many of those companies would receive public support today?

The doors to these 'tax optimisations' should be closed once and for all, especially now during the pandemic. Closing them would provide our authorities with resources for investment in health and elder care, education, science, and culture.

Further, there is the issue of government participation in the governance of the companies in which they invest for 'bail-out' purposes. The German government has invested nine billion euros in Lufthansa, i.e., nearly twice the value of its market capitalization. The government could have just bought the company outright. At the very least, the government could have been expected to have a say in the direction of the company. This did not happen. In exchange, the government acquired a mere one-fifth of the shares, which did not even secure it a blocking minority. Nor did it obtain a degree of participation that would have enabled it to prevent Lufthansa from cutting thousands of jobs and further lowering wages. Can this really be true? Surely a government, whose monies come from the people, cannot invest nine billion euros into a company and then be left with very little influence to exert? If we're all going to pay, we should have our say.

* * *

Countries are different from each other, and one agreement may be better than the other, but everywhere the underlying idea is the same: continue with 'business as usual', with or without pollution, with or without tax avoidance. Whereas now a shift is needed in order to enforce different strategic choices. Will the government loosen the purse strings? It will, but then with a new set of rules.

Let's put an end to the long-standing trend of reducing corporate taxes for multinationals. Governments allow themselves to be fleeced and the ultimate victims are nurses, teachers, bus and tram drivers, and other essential workers.

President Trump granted big business and billionaires a massive tax-cut in 2017. *The New York Times* stated that the tax-cut resulted in 5.5 trillion euros in tax relief to the richest Americans and companies. Unbelievable! This is more than what the US government is spending on emergency aid today. This sentence bears re-reading. The tax cuts, signed into law by Trump for US multinationals, amounted to more than what has been allocated today for emergency relief.

One would expect, given these dire economic conditions, that the tax cut will be rolled back soon, thus allowing the US government to pay off some debt and provide economic aid to all Americans. Millions of Americans would then be able to pay their rent or mortgage and they would not have to line up at food banks. The influence exerted by capital on politics is devastating. Yet, the US 'rescue' plans under Trump provided additional tax gifts to the biggest of the big. Major profiteers from the tax-shift in 2017 were given another handout from the US government. Can this be called the superiority of the private market?

Is All That Money Going to Those Who Need It?

Prophets of the private market are chattering on Twitter that there is no money to invest. In the meantime, however, public money is sloshing around. It is not so much a question of whether there is money, as where it should go.

We do not need government support to destroy jobs. Subsidies should not be granted to help the fossil fuels sector. The credit lines of central banks should not be used to buy shares, enter into mergers, or distribute dividends.

A Plan Like the One Proposed by

Alexandria Ocasio-Cortez

There is an old saying: kill two birds with one stone. When faced with the threat of two looming major crises, one would have to be a fool not to deal with them together if possible. Its's a man-on-the-moon moment. 'The moment of truth' sounds much more prosaic in Dutch.

What two crises? The economic downturn and climate change – the other pandemic that is bound to overwhelm us if we do nothing.

With the exception of a few climate negationists – often the same deniers who, at the onset of the COVID-19 crisis, were spouting hot air on 'this pandemic' – everyone is in agreement: it's time to act now. It's raining Green Deals, some more detailed than others. Two diverging perceptions, however, are underlying all of them and they are fundamentally different.

The dominant view is that we need to donate a massive amount of public money to large private businesses that will then use these funds to make the ecological and digital transition. This vision is defended, among others, by European big industry, united in Business Europe. They are counting on European funding to become the 'European champions' of ecological transition and digitisation. The European Commission listens to them. It wants to mobilise a combined one trillion euros for a Green Deal and speaks of 'a new industrial strategy for a globally competitive, green, and digital Europe'.

The other view is that these funds should be used to realize public investments, which would allow the keys to ecological and digital transformation to remain in public hands. We would then

A Plan Like the One Proposed by AOC

be able to set the objectives publicly and control each step, so that capital is not secreted away into the stock market or speculation.

The inspiration for this comes from the Green New Deal submitted to the US Congress by Alexandria Ocasio-Cortez, also known by her initials AOC. She is the youngest woman ever to serve in the United States Congress. With her working-class background, she is an outsider in the Congress. But both friend and foe have a taste for her fresh and flamboyant true-speak. She wears her heart on her sleeve. She learned that in the working-class neighbourhoods of the Bronx in New York, where she once made a living as a waitress and bartender.

In February 2019, AOC, together with Senator Bernie Sanders, submitted her Green New Deal. The two of them want the government to take back the helm of the fight against climate change as the fossil giants have caused so much damage. The goal is 100% renewable electricity and mobility by 2030. AOC wants sixteen trillion dollars mobilized for this purpose. Public ownership of the entire production and distribution network would be placed under the control of five regional Power Authority Administrations. Her plan also includes ambitious measures that focus on renovation loans to insulate homes and buildings for families, the self-employed, and small business. This would reduce energy consumption. Thanks to this plan, as many as twenty million new jobs could be created. It modeled itself on the New Deal with which President Roosevelt tackled the Great Depression in the 1930s.

This is the choice with which we are faced. We can choose to dole out public money to serve private giants and continue to have trust in market forces. This is the option chosen by almost all political parties, including most green parties, in one variant or another, with more or less control of how the funds are used. Or we can choose to invest as a government, impose our own public-based objectives, and create sustainable jobs.

* * *

In 1988, NASA researcher James Hansen was the first to link global warming to greenhouse gas emissions resulting from human activity. That was more than thirty years ago. To date, we have been unable to achieve any progress against this unfettered destruction of our planet. We have put our fate in the hands of profit-mongers and are obstinately continuing to trust the 'free' market; it is almost a religion. Emissions have been increasing and the atmosphere has continued to warm, with the disastrous consequences as predicted. AOC's plan is inspiring because it has abandoned that logic at last.

It is a matter of urgency: the COVID-19 pandemic, the impending recession, and the pace of climate change are linked together and growing. There is hope, however. It is precisely in times of crisis that everything starts shifting and moving, including what until then seemed steady as a rock.

In Lisbon, on 1 November, 1755, a deadly, destructive earthquake struck. What was that? The earthquake was followed by a tidal wave in the low-lying districts of the city, and in the upper suburbs a fire that reduced everything to ashes. The trauma led people to cast doubt on the entire feudal order. The earthquake was followed by a mindquake, Philipp Blom writes in a beautiful essay.

Both back then and today, an ideologically and widely shared concept of the world was plunged into crisis by an external shock. In those days, the omnipotent statue of an omniscient god fell from its pedestal and was replaced by the Enlightenment. Today the 'question of the market's omnipotence' has been raised, writes Blom. He continues, 'For decades, people seeking an alternative to the suicidal hypercapitalism that the developed world maintains have been told that there is no such alternative, that there is no better way to run things, that they already live in the best of all possible worlds.' He is convinced that the debate will accompany us for decades to come, that it will proliferate 'on the ruins of the liberal vision that sees a society as a market.'

Today's mindquake should give us a new vision, coherence, and a roadmap for fast, decisive, and ambitious action. A return to public initiatives is the only structural way out in the short term. Such a step would allow us both to abandon inefficient and anti-social market mechanisms in climate policy, and to build a new ecological infrastructure. We would ban the market from the social sectors, which would enable us to invest in prevention, healthcare, and housing.

COVID-19 doesn't care about boundaries. The outbreak in Lombardy magnified the fact that many problems can be better tackled at a European level. Scale is important. This is the case for climate issues, major infrastructure works, energy, and mobility. For instance, we need trans-European hydrogen pipelines and new continental rail links to replace short-haul flights. It is also advantageous in every respect from a broad European perspective to focus on the rollout of a high-performance digital network, which should protect data and privacy against marketeers and other high-jackers.

The COVID-19 mindquake has shaken the 'all-powerful market'. Dare to think outside the box! Why shouldn't European public consortiums be established? Pan-European production and management companies, such as Airbus, should be fully publicly-owned. Airbus is a European company with the participation of several countries, and with production departments spread across the continent. Why not think about public consortiums for energy, for transport, for the digital transition, for healthcare?

The Prometheus Plan

Never before had Prometheus put Zeus, the supreme god, to the test; he went ahead with his plan and he brought fire to man. No matter how dear Zeus was to him, he still preferred mankind. Prometheus went from village to village and taught man the techniques of forging metal, making pots, and roasting meat. Prometheus was a drifter, a man of technology, and a friend to humans. His name means 'the far-sighted'.

This moment necessitates a forward-looking plan based on today's technical know-how. This is why I call it a Prometheus plan. It incorporates four elements: not the water, earth, air, and fire of the ancient Greeks, but energy, transport, the digital sector, and healthcare.

Many might say that it is precisely all this technology and all this fire that have brought about so much evil. The evil has not been brought about by technology itself, but by the use capitalism has made of it. Capitalism sacrifices almost everything on the altar of profit. Capital holds nothing sacred; Marx described that 150 years ago.

'If we could somehow overcome our selfishness, we would notice that new microbes kept quietly to their niche; they would have stayed there if we had not destroyed their natural shelter' says Italian writer Paolo Giordani.

'Because of our aggressive behaviour towards the environment, we are brought more and more into contact with these new pathogens, which were, until recently, confined to their natural niches. Deforestation brings us closer to habitats that did not count on our presence. The accelerating extinction of many animal species is forcing the bacteria living in their insides to relocate.

Intensive livestock farming creates unintentional breeding grounds where literally everything is growing rampant.'

In the spirit of Greek mythology, it could well be that Nemesis, the goddess of vengeance, introduced COVID-19 into one of Pandora's jars to punish mankind for its arrogance, hubris in Greek.

This arrogance belongs to a system that makes everything that lives and moves marketable. A system that can no longer look at man or nature without seeing figures and profitability. Just like the inner fire that makes us think, dream, and act, technology and science per se are friends of mankind. Let's be grateful to Prometheus for this. The issue at stake is how to put all this knowledge to good use; not to mismanage it in order to make profits from everything.

Our goal should be to live together on this planet and to keep the planet livable. Our Prometheus plan is in line with the needs of man and nature, not with the wishes of profit and the stock market.

* * *

Energy is the first element. We have now arrived at a crossroads: are we going to move from a fossil fuel economy to a renewable-energy economy, or not?

We need to move towards a new, technologically very different energy model. The current one is centralised; it depends on large nuclear and gas power plants and supplies a constant amount of electricity. The new model is local, runs on renewable energy, and takes peaks and troughs into account. The network is different in the new model, it has to be operated intelligently and storage capacity (based on hydrogen as energy carrier) plays an essential role in the management of those peaks and troughs.

The problem is that these two models are mutually exclusive. As long as we rely on the traditional energy supply from large nuclear and gas-fired power stations, the new model will not be able to break through. In order to make the breakthrough possible, though, we need an investment push from Europe. Since there is a lot of public money at stake here, we would be well advised to make it a public project.

Let's bring all the great minds together, centralise the best technologies, and develop a broad European vision in a joint European energy consortium. Such a step will enable us to make large-scale continental investments. President Roosevelt did just that when he proposed a vast road network. We have to develop energy networks that will run on offshore wind farms on the Atlantic and the Baltic sides of the continent and solar panel fields on the Mediterranean side, for example. By developing intelligent networks, we can ensure the establishment of local, decentralised energy networks. This is already the case today in Munich and other urban areas. It allows for a fine interweaving of local and global benefits. By investing European money in this, we can create tens of thousands of new and sustainable jobs.

* * *

Transport is the second element of the Prometheus plan. A lot of public money goes to the rescue of large private airlines. There is no vision for the development of a European transport infrastructure. Railway companies are regularly put up for sale, ports are engaged in ruthless competition, and travelling throughout the continent is cheaper by plane than by train.

Public transport is a decisive factor in the mobility transition. A model needs to be created where public transport is present, reliable, punctual, safe, comfortable, efficient, and affordable; it is the only way to avoid excessive private transport and the associated traffic jams and pollution. Electric cars are not going to provide a sustainable solution to the existing problems. Very scarce raw materials such as lithium, cobalt, and nickel are essential in batteries used in this type of car. It is not healthy.

Our Prometheus plan envisages a European public transport

consortium, which would invest in the expansion of railways and green public transport and in additional railway infrastructure, trains, trams, and environmentally friendly buses, minibuses, and shared cars.

This second pillar can also create thousands of sustainable jobs. It can put to work the available know-how, techniques, and people from the severely affected automotive sector.

* * *

The third element is the digital sector. E-working was and continues to be extensive during lockdowns. E-working runs digitally, as do video meetings and platform encounters. E-commerce has gone through the roof as well, unfortunately at the detriment of local producers and traders. Underpaid couriers often had to carry on working without protection in the heat of the pandemic. That's what I was talking about in the first part of this book. Amazon boss Jeff Bezos has benefited from all this misery and in no small way indeed. Over just a couple of months, his personal assets have grown by thirty-five billion dollars. Bezos, now the richest man on earth, is worth $186 billion. That is more than the national income of Hungary, the Ukraine, or Qatar.

At the end of July 2020, the richest man on earth was put on the spot by the American Congress, together with the bosses of Google, Facebook, and Apple. Congress wanted to question them about the imperial monopoly power they are exercising to strangle emerging players. The tech-keepers reacted with irresponsible chatter: 'No, we're not that powerful, we're just vulnerable birds in a big and ruthless world market.' The hearing led nowhere.

This did not make the stakes less important. The digital shift is a true industrial revolution – the fourth. It is based on artificial intelligence, the cloud, and especially big data. A European digital consortium could bring about that change and keep the data public. In that context, Europe's top specialists would work together to make this digital revolution available for public rather than narrow corporate interests. Developing new technologies aimed at finding solutions in terms of mobility, logistics, communication, the environment, and human working conditions is a mobilizing project that will appeal to tens of thousands of young people.

* * *

The fourth element is care. In the broad sense, human care. In the past thirty years, much has been destroyed regarding human care. We need to put in place a different structure. We are talking here about the transition to a preventive health system, which was the subject-matter of the second part of this book. Such a shift will allow us to be better prepared to prevent epidemics and to keep a finger on the pulse of our neighbourhoods with prevention healthcare workers; similar to what Kerala (India) has created, but in Europe. It will be local development with a comprehensive vision.

This approach is necessary in the field of elderly care as well. The picture of the silver multinationals with their hundreds of rest homes, where thousands of care providers are subjected to a policy aimed at squeezing out every penny in order to achieve a 15% return has no future. We know now that elderly care thrives locally, on a smaller scale, not isolated from the human world, but integrated into local life.

The Prometheus plan contains a vision for a European public consortium for research, development, and innovation in health care. This should ensure that we focus on the development of essential vaccines and drugs that will subsequently be stocked in sufficient amounts and made available to everyone, of course.

The prevention approach is intended to result in particular attention being paid to healthy living conditions. As part of a global approach, local public construction consortiums can provide insulation to millions of homes, small businesses, schools, and public buildings with a third-party payer scheme. Just as Alexandria Ocasio-Cortez has suggested in her plan. It is good for the climate, for your wallet, and for your health. These consortiums can also provide many new homes based on the Vienna model: the Austrian capital's programme for modern, sustainable, and affordable housing. In this way, urbanization programmes take shape at the same time as the issues of ghettoisation and social inequality are tackled. During lockdown, the latter have been getting worse.

This plan is a vast new project that needs the participation of tens of thousands of people.

* * *

The four elements of our Prometheus plan ensure new economic activities with their own dynamics: companies specialized in renewable energy, insulation, and public transport, a thriving construction and renovation sector, niche companies for social assistance and care, and so on. These are all activities that cannot be delocalized. They are good for hundreds of thousands of new jobs.

The massive public investment foreseen in the Prometheus plan is only possible if we move away from the European principles of competition. This would allow us to reinstate public monopolies: in energy, transport, digitisation, care, and lending. The commercialisation of care has caused havoc, as has the commercialisation of energy and transport. Governments must take the initiative to make this plan a reality. European treaties that prevent this should be scrapped.

The same applies to the European austerity treaties. Both the Stability and Growth Pact and the Fiscal Compact are now temporarily suspended. Let's repeal them for good. And with this, the anti-social European Semester mechanism, the 'structural reforms' of which have paved the way for the dismantlement of pensions, wages, and public services. We will put all that behind us.

In 1948, with Europe in ruins after twelve years of fascism

and five years of war, a Reconstruction Bank was established in Germany, the Kreditanstalt für Wiederaufbau (KfW). The Germans knew then that strategic investments were best kept out of the current budget. These strategic investments were financed with loans, which were amortized over time. It is with this in mind that the KfW, a public investment bank active in financing large housing and infrastructure projects, was set up.

In order to build a sustainable and social world on what is emerging from the ruins of the crisis, we need to invest. We need loans to do this, just like in 1948 Germany. In addition to a European Recovery Plan, we need a European Reconstruction Fund, which will provide loans exclusively to European projects in the energy, transport, digitization, and healthcare sectors, i.e., to the public consortiums that will be in charge of implementing them.

Start-up capital is needed to set up such a fund. The agreement of 21 July 2020 implies that Europe will soon tentatively collect taxes itself. What is envisaged is a tax on disposable plastic or an energy tax. With the Workers' Party of Belgium, we tend to think more of a European tax on wealth, a proposal that is getting increasingly wide support. Part of the proceeds from such a tax could be used to set up the Reconstruction Fund. Working capital can be obtained from savings mobilised by the fund, as the KfW does in Germany, through issuing state-guaranteed bonds. Ultimately, every euro invested will yield two. There will be less waste, less pollution, more employment, better salaries, better care, and a health bonus thanks to a better environment. These are all financial returns on investment.

Making Circumstances Human

Sometimes everything runs at an excruciatingly slow speed. And then, all of a sudden, it gains momentum, just like now. The pandemic has caused many dominoes to fall. We are going through turbulent times; we are sitting right in the middle of a shock wave that is far from over.

'The old world is dying; the new world announces itself. In this interregnum, a great variety of morbid symptoms appear' Italian communist writer Antonio Gramsci wrote.

Here they are, the monsters, right in front of us. It is the fault of the Chinese; it is the fault of the Moroccans; it is the fault of the working-class neighbourhoods; or it is the fault of the canaille. It is called shifting-the-blame. While stock exchanges were going through the roof and multi-multi-millionaires were adding obscene amounts to their wealth, the extreme right organized a blame game among the people. People were pointing the finger at each other and those at the top were laughing up their sleeves. 'We must take care of our own people' they called out against a virus that knows neither language nor boundaries.

In Belgium, the Vlaams Belang has approved all cost-saving measures in the healthcare sector for three decades now, just like the extreme right throughout Europe. Their noble members of the European Parliament systematically vote not only against any proposal on wealth taxation, but also against tackling tax fraud. Their colleagues from the Le Pen party in France and from the Salvini Lega party in Italy are doing exactly the same. The 'yes' button is activated when commercialisation and privatisation of healthcare are put on the table. The 'no' button is pressed when major fraud or fortunes are at stake.

In December 2019, VB leader Tom Van Grieken received

the Lega guru Matteo Salvini as a rock star at the Antwerp Handelsbeurs. Salvini was considered to be the example to follow for the whole of Europe. Six months later, the Lombards were licking their wounds. Lombardy is governed by Attilio Fontana, Salvini's party colleague in the Lega. He made a mess of it all. Judicial inquiries against him are ongoing today. An investigation into the dubious decision to send COVID-19 patients from hospitals back to residential care centres against medical advise is ongoing, as is an investigation into alleged fraud relating to the delivery of 70,000 protective overalls by his brother-in-law. In the course of their duties, investigators ran into funds belonging to Fontana via accounts in the Bahamas and Switzerland.

The extreme right does not break with privatisation and liberalisation policies. It takes those policies to the extreme and makes people bitter, submissive, and accusatory of others. This is written in the booklet of the VB MPs Barbara Pas and Chris Janssens: It is the fault of Belgium; it is China's fault; and it is the World Health Organization's fault. Going so far as to say that in spite of the many 'right' decisions he has made, Trump is misunderstood as a leader.

The lid is kept closed, however, on the consequences of those allegedly correct decisions. The same is happening in Brazil where Bolsonaro, the other hero of the extreme right, is producing a catastrophe. In mid-July 2020, the well-known Brazilian theologian Frei Betto, brought a sharp charge against Bolsonaro. 'Dear friends, a genocide is taking place in Brazil,' he declared. He was writing about 'the general indifference of the Bolsonaro government,' while at the same time eighty thousand corpses had already been buried. Neither in Lombardy, nor in Brazil, nor in the United States, nowhere is the extreme right part of the solution. It is an integral part of the problem.

* * *

'We must turn suffering into strength', stated Doctor Vittorio

Agnoletto's in his acclaimed speech in Milan on 20 June 2020, in the Piazza del Duomo. Health professionals and grassroot organisations had come together: 'Salviamo La Lombardia', let's save Lombardy.

Turning suffering into strength is not easy to do, because the virus is circulating 'right and left' at the same time. This is not really so because the virus is the virus, period. This is a quip, a shrewd comparison made by French filmmaker François Ruffin in his fiery book 'Leur Folie, Nos Vies'.

The virus is a right-winger because it separates us, it throws us back on our heels. Living space is too cramped; stress is too high; and domestic violence is on the increase. Suspicion is creeping into society and some 'baddy' even launched the term social distancing. Social distancing? Physical distancing, that's OK, one and a half meters. But why social distancing? Nay, not even one millimeter. Social distancing means mental doom.

'The Solitude of Prime Numbers' is Paolo Giordano's bestseller. Today the author is writing about solitude again. '[There is] the solitude of a person in intensive care who has to communicate with others through a glass panel. There is another kind of solitude, though, quite impalpable: the loneliness of tightly pursed lips behind mouth masks, suspicious glances, compulsory lockdown. In times of contagion, we are all both free and under house arrest.'

Nobody likes being excluded. Even if you know it is only going to be temporary, it makes you suffer. 'We have the irrepressible need to be with others, to be among people. Similar to the need to breathe', the Italian writer understands.

The comparison continues: this virus is also a left-winger. We take care of each other. We need each other. Never was 'the other' so important as in this pandemic loneliness. We engage 'the other' doing our shopping, putting teddy bears in front of the windows, colouring rainbows, playing the accordion in front of residential care centres, writing messages for garbage collectors, sticking encouraging notes for package deliverers on the mailboxes, helping kids with homework, collecting laptops, sewing tons of masks, baking cakes, you name it. All over the world there has been a big surge in creativity – from the bottom up, as usual. This is the way new cooperatives and new neighbourhood councils are created. Solidarity on a large or small scale is the expression of socialist values: mutual aid, solidarity, cooperation, collectivism, mutual respect, unity between word and deed, respect for work, sense of initiative, and internationalism – deeds, not words.

This is how concepts, which have been prohibited until yesterday, spring to life again. Public initiatives as alternatives to market-driven initiatives are developed. Health and welfare instead of economic interests are prioritized. A planned approach instead of the tale of deregulation of markets is enforced. Social security becomes a cathedral to replace the old-fashioned debit entry.

You'll Never Walk Alone: the song was played on the morning of 20 March 2020 at a quarter to nine on all European radios. It was a goosebumps moment for the text was so appropriate. Three days later, the Belgian newspaper *Het Laatste Nieuws* asked thousands of their fellow countrymen: 'What is the most important thing in times of crisis?' The answer was not 'money'. Nine out of ten Belgians answered: 'solidarity'.

* * *

Nothing, however, is free in life and the future will be a battleground. We must be able to hold on to the heat of the moment. The current discourse needs to be recorded; images need to be etched in our minds. Because soon they will want us to forget everything: body bags piled up in residential care centres; mountains of destroyed stocks of masks thrown into trash bins; criminal negligence perpetrated by government officials; squabbles in parliaments that never provide the needy with help; and the exposé of the absurdity of confederalism. They will want us to forget the total failure of the self-regulating market; the cost cutting in the hospitals; the failure to develop vaccines; the simultaneous increase of hunger and wealth in the world; and the obscene parties on the stock market.

The heroes will be asked to forget that they are heroes. When this happens, we will play the whole movie all over again, and we will not allow all this suffering to have been in vain.

Doctor Dirk Van Duppen died at the start of this pandemic. For years, he had been a friend and comrade in arms, an inspirer of Medicine for the People. Dirk liked to quote Portuguese writer José Saramago: 'If man is shaped by circumstances, then we must shape those circumstances humanely.'

We know that today it is possible to guarantee everyone a secure and dignified life. We know that today it is possible to overcome need and misery worldwide. We know that people are able to live in dignity, to be independent, aware, and supportive. We need a society that allows people to be human again. We need a new brand of socialism.

Such a prospect is utopia and reality at the same time. Utopia, because we are in a grey zone between the old world and the new one, and because righteousness still seems a long way off. Utopia, because those in power want to dismiss any systemic alternative as impossible to realize and because the mindquake has yet to be pushed through to its fullest. Reality, because there is no alternative for man and our planet other than a world run on a human scale.

Let us make circumstances human.

The future belongs to those who are keeping the world running.

Antwerp, 31 July 2020.

www.ingramcontent.com/pod-product-compliance
Lightning Source LLC
Chambersburg PA
CBHW020029040426
42333CB00039B/707